PRESCHOOL LESSON PLANS

J. HOBBS

Printed in the United States of America
First Printing 2020
First Edition 2020

10 9 8 7 6 5 4 3 2 1

Table of Contents

Preschool Lesson Plans

These preschool lesson plans evolved from years of experience. I was in search of a curriculum that provided engaging, developmentally appropriate experiences to build a firm base for future learning. I wanted plans that would spark curiosity, questions, and exploration. I also wanted to do this with materials that are natural, affordable, easy to access, or that could be found at home. That is exactly what the preschool lesson plans do! Each week provides students with a full week of learning and exploration. The lessons do not take much planning but allow for ample opportunities to ask questions and engage in meaningful conversation. This book of plans can be used in a group setting or easily adapted for homeschool. I hope you enjoy these activities as much as my students have over the years! Below is a brief explanation of the activities provided in this book. These activities can be flexible and used to fit your program or homeschool.

Transition

Transition is the time of the day when students must move from one activity/location to another. This is a perfect teachable moment! The teacher will use a transition activity such as "Everyone wearing the color blue, please line up" or "All girls line up." The transition activity teaches a skill/concept and provides an organized transition.

Extension Center

The extension activity is designed to carry over concepts, projects, or ideas that may be of interest to the students. This activity also allows the teacher and students to expand on an idea for deeper understanding and higher-level questioning. You will want to create an indoor/outdoor center for this activity.

Provocation

Provocations stimulate thoughts, discussions, questions, interests, creativity, and ideas. Materials are arranged in an aesthetically pleasing way to draw attention and provoke creativity. Provocations can come in many forms:

- Old classroom materials displayed in a new way
- Nature elements available for arrangement and manipulation
- Pictures or books open to a specific page along with materials for creation
- A vase of flowers for inspiration along with paper and paints to create

Morning Meeting

The **morning meeting** should be a happy gathering and greeting to begin the day. This meeting sets the tone for the rest of the day in terms of expectations, gratitude, respect, and overall attitude for students and teachers. Begin your meeting with your favorite **gathering song**.

This song should stay the same throughout the year to build a routine. When children hear the song, they should know that it signifies gathering together at a designated place in your classroom or home.

Morning Message

The Monday **Morning Message** should already be written and will be read by the teacher. The teacher should point to the words as he/she reads them. The lesson plans will indicate the letter/word/punctuation focus. This should be interactive by choosing students to come and circle the letter, word, etc.

Once the letter has been recognized, the teacher should demonstrate the letter sound, have students repeat the sound, and then ask students to think of words that begin with that sound. Write two words each day on a word chart. Hang chart paper up each week to create a word list under the letter.

My News

My News is simply asking the students if they have any news to share. Only choose 3–5 students daily. Write their message on chart paper in one sentence and add their name at the end. Leave two lines between each child's sentence for later use. Try to find a way to incorporate the letter of the week into this sentence (most of the time, this can be done without much thought).

Learning Centers/Free Choice

Learning centers/free choice is an integral part of the day. This is where students choose their activity and discover their interests. During this time, the STEAM project, writing, sensory, process art, and learning centers are available as choices for the student if not completed during a rotation during the day or as a daily activity for homeschool. We encourage students to participate in projects, writing and discovering new things, but we do not force or dictate the center they must be in. A child learns when he/she is in a receptive mode, meaning when he/she is comfortable, interested, and relaxed. This should evolve over time. Centers should include but are not limited to dramatic play, writing, blocks, music/dance, science, sensory, art, manipulatives, puzzles, and library. There should be centers that can host only one child and centers that can host multiple children at one time. This is a time when the teacher should listen to the students, ask questions, demonstrate counting, patterning, compare objects, and encourage curiosity. There is a space on the lesson plans for you to write in any changes or additions you make to centers. For example, this may be adding fall leaves to the science center or spring raincoats/boots to the dramatic play.

STEM/STEAM Projects

The **STEAM projects** should be conducted in a small group. The projects are cross-curricular, providing problem-solving and critical thinking over several subject areas at once.

S=Science   T=Technology   E=Engineering   A=Art   M=Math

Outdoor Time

Outdoor time is a vital piece of education. Students require time to run free, explore, get oxygen into their bodies, and enjoy nature. Your time outside should involve gross motor activities such as running, climbing, jumping, swinging, and skipping. Nature is the perfect classroom and offers endless learning opportunities. Depending on your play space, you may want to involve the children in gardening, watering plants, weeding, etc. Sensory activities, such as sand and water play, are perfect for the outdoors. The outdoors is also the perfect host for messy art and science activities.

Process Art

Process art is a child-led experience. The materials should be available for a child to choose what they want to create and how they want to create it. Children can be taught boundaries during this time, such as how much of a material can be used or where and what is appropriate to paint, draw, or color on. Process art should be open-ended, calming, joyful, and result in unique pieces for each child who participates. The art does not have step-by-step instructions, but rather encourages the child to use his/her creativity.

Story Time

Story time is the cozy downtime when your preschool family comes together. Stories should be developmentally appropriate for the age group you are teaching. The teacher should use animation, projection, and intonation when reading a story. So much can be taught during this short time, such as social skills, author, illustrator, prediction, characters, setting, reading from left to right, turning pages, beginning, middle, end, etc. These skills will be noted in your lesson plans. Skills should be discussed before and after reading, so as not to interrupt the story.

Writing

The **writing** center is taken from the **My News** activity, which occurs during the **morning meeting.** Cut the news into strips for the children, providing each child with their strip of news to work on. Read the student's my news to them while pointing at each word. Have them find the letter of the week in their news. Highlight the letter/word you want them to practice. Have them trace the highlighted letter/word. Then the child should try and write the letter/word on the blank line below their message. The child should also trace and write their name.

Word of the Week

The **Word of the Week** will be used in the **Morning Message,** and it can also be used in **My News.** The Word of the Week should be laminated and placed in the writing center for children to see, copy, and explore throughout the week.

Sensory

Sensory is any activity that stimulates a child's senses (touch, taste, sight, smell, feel). These activities are designed to create curiosity, exploration, discovery, and creation. Sensory activities naturally encourage a child to use scientific processes while they play and investigate.

Calendar Activity

Calendar activities are a bit of a tradition in many preschools. There are so many "Days of the Week" and "Months of the Year" songs that you can find online! The calendar activities are an effective and fun way to teach math skills. The calendar activities are broken down to small pieces each day, so students will not get bored with too much repetition. The lesson plans incorporate a variety of movements and patterns to create a developmentally appropriate learning environment. You may also create special days such as "Upside-Down Hug Thursdays" or "Gardening Fridays." You can buy or make a calendar to place on the wall or refrigerator if you are homeschooling.

Music and Movement

Music and movement are great teaching tools. Music inspires and encourages creative movement along with fostering listening and language skills such as vocabulary and rhyming. You will want to add your favorite songs to represent your classroom's interest. Every preschooler has their favorite song to sing and dance to!

Parent Letter

The Parent Letter is the teacher or nanny's way of communicating what is happening in the classroom or at home. This lets the parents know what their child is learning and what is available to their child each day. The Parent Letter gives parents the opportunity to talk with their child about what is happening at school and hopefully continue/encourage that same learning at home. It is also a resource for the teacher. The Parent Letter asks parents to bring in supplies they may have readily available, such as toilet paper rolls, glass jars, etc. This creates a community atmosphere while fulfilling a need in the classroom.

Letter and Word Order

The **letters** are presented in an order that allows for the teaching of the preschool Dolch word list to build up vocabulary.

Assessment

The **Assessment Tool** is provided in a document separate from the Lesson Plans. This tool should be used on an observational basis rather than pulling children aside. The lesson plans indicate (under the 'Documentation' column) times in which a teacher may observe the skills on the assessment. An assessment should be created for each child in the class. The teacher should keep the tool readily available, so as not to create a large amount of work at the end of a semester. We suggest leaving these tools in folders that parents can access throughout the year rather than just two or three times a year.

This creates an ongoing conversation with parents and helps them to understand where their child is developmentally without the stress of waiting for results at a parent-teacher conference.

Documentation

The **Documentation** column signifies two things: 1) The activity may provide an opportunity to observe a student at work on a skill found in the assessment tool, and 2) The activity may provide an opportunity to take a picture for documentation. These pictures can be used for a child's portfolio and/or an end-of-the-year video.

Homeschool Setting

Preschool lesson plans are perfect for homeschooling your 3–5-year-old. The weekly lesson plans are packed full of fun, educational, and open-ended activities for your child. The activities are open-ended enough to do with children of different ages.

Here are a few steps to make using the preschool lesson plans fast, easy, fun, and effective:

1. Read through the weekly plans the week before you plan to implement them.
2. Print off the **Shopping List** and gather all materials into a designated basket or box.
3. Use the chart below to plan your week

*The "x" marks the days you should implement the activity

HOMESCHOOL
WEEKLY SCHEDULE & PLANS

ACTIVITY	Day 1	Day 2	Day 3	Day 4	Day 5
Morning Meeting	x		x		
Calendar Time		x		x	
Process Art	x				
Writing		x		x	
Provocation		x			
STEAM			x		
Sensory				x	
Story Time	x	x	x	x	x
Field Trip/Free Day *Not provided by PK					x
Spiritual/Motivational *Not provided by PK	x		x		x

DAILY SCHEDULE & PLANS

STANDARDS	TIME	ACTIVITY	MATERIALS	DOCUMENTATION
Cognitive Development Language Development	------	**Weekly Transition:** Colors (i.e., if you have the color red on, please line up) - hold up color cards or crayons for transition times.	Color cards or crayons	Assessment photo
Cognitive Development		**Extension Center:** *What was successful and interesting to students last week? Carry this over to a center this week so that the students may extend this play/learning.*		Assessment photo
Cognitive Development		**Provocation:** Set out sticks, stones, and blocks in a designated space for building and design. Use the materials to build a couple of designs for demonstration. Then encourage the students to explore the materials and build something of their own	Sticks, stones, blocks	Assessment photo
Cognitive Development Language Development Fine Motor Development Home Connection		**Morning Meeting:** 1. Good morning song (teacher's choice) 2. Monday: Morning Message **Letter/word focus:** D, d 3. Tues–Fri: **My News** - Talk with the students and write down one short sentence that he/she says (i.e., "I like playing in the mud." —Annie)	Music device, whiteboard, chart paper, Sharpie, dry-erase marker	Assessment photo

STANDARDS	TIME	OUTDOOR ACTIVITIES	MATERIALS	DOCUMENTATION
Cognitive Development Language Development Sensory Development Gross Motor Development		**Outdoor Time/Free Choice:** *Optional activities include: watering plants, pulling weeds, gardening, sensory, snow painting, snowman building, snow shoveling, raking leaves, etc.*		Assessment photo
		Extra Activities:		

7

STANDARDS	TIME	LEARNING CENTER ACTIVITY CHOICES	MATERIALS	DOCUMENTATION
Cognitive Development Language Development Fine Motor Development Home Connection		**Writing:** Name, letter focus, My News. Use relevant writing sheets to complete writing time or allow the students time to freely draw and the teacher to dictate the students' drawings.	Highlighter, pencils, or crayons	Assessment photo
Cognitive Development Sensory Development		**Sensory:** Place sand, dinosaurs, and rocks in the sensory bin for exploration.	Sand, dinosaurs, rocks	Assessment photo
Cognitive Development Language Development Fine Motor Development Sensory Development Gross Motor Development		**Learning Centers:** *Note any changes and/or additions made to learning centers.*		Assessment photo
Cognitive Development Language Development Fine Motor Development Sensory Development		**Process Art:** Place a variety of cut-out shapes on the table along with construction paper and glue for children to explore and create. When the child finishes their piece of art, ask him/her to tell you about it. Dictate his/her words onto the art.	Construction paper, shape cut-outs, glue, paint brushes for glue, Sharpie	Assessment photo
Cognitive Development Language Development Fine Motor Development Sensory Development		**Question:** What is an explosion? **View:** Use the Internet to view a volcano explosion or read a book about volcanoes. **STEAM:** Give each child a plate, a small Dixie cup, and some clay/playdough. Let them build their own volcano around the small cup. Now it's time for the explosion. Let children pour in the ingredients: ½ cup of vinegar, couple drops of dish soap, and 4 Tbsp baking soda. Finally, discover what happens!	Paper plates, small cups, clay, paint, vinegar, dish soap, baking soda	Assessment photo

STANDARDS	TIME	CIRCLE TIME ACTIVITIES	MATERIALS	DOCUMENTATION
Cognitive Development Language Development Gross Motor Development		Circle Time: 1. Calendar activities (days, months, counting, number patterns, season, year). -Jump while counting the days of the month 2. Music and movement:	Calendar, colored calendar numbers, music source	Assessment photo
Cognitive Development Language Development		Story Time: Non-fiction books related to Volcanoes, explosions, and/or scientists		Assessment photo

STANDARDS	TIME	EXTRA ACTIVITIES	MATERIALS	DOCUMENTATION

1. Relevant Writing 1

Name Recognition and Practice

_____

Letter Recognition and Practice

D_____

d_____

1. Relevant Writing 2

My News

*Write the student's news on the line below using a highlighter.

_____ •

*Encourage student to draw a picture of their news below.

1. Week 1 Shopping List

ITEMS	YES, we have this item	NO, we need to buy	$ COST of item	ITEMS	YES, we have this item	NO, we need to buy	$ COST of item
PROVOCATION: Sticks Stone Blocks				**SENSORY:** Sand Dinosaurs Rocks			
MORNING MEETING: Music device Whiteboard/chart paper Sharpie/dry erase marker Dry erase marker				**PROCESS ART:** Construction paper Shape cut-outs Glue Paint brushes for gluing Sharpie			
WRITING: Highlighter Chart paper/chalkboard/dry erase board Pencils				**STEAM:** Paper plates Dixie cups Clay Paint Vinegar Dish soap Baking soda			

1. Parent Letter

Dear Family,

This week your preschooler will be exploring the world of explosions! What child doesn't love explosions? The preschoolers will experiment with building volcanoes and making them erupt. You may even explode something at home! If so, the class would love to hear about it or see a video of your explosion.

Provocation: Stick & stone building	Sensory: The Dinosaur Sanctuary	Letter/Word Focus: D, d
Process Art: Shapes	STEM Project: Explosions & volcanoes	Writing: My News, letter D, d, name

DAILY SCHEDULE & PLANS

STANDARDS	TIME	DAILY ACTIVITIES	MATERIALS	DOCUMENTATION
Cognitive Development Language Development	------	**Weekly Transition:** Age (i.e., if you are four years old, please line up.) Use your fingers or a number card as a visual.		Assessment
Cognitive Development	------	**Extension Center:** *What was successful and interesting to students last week? Carry this over to a center this week so that the students may extend this play/learning.*		Assessment photo
Cognitive Development		**Provocation:** Write each child's name on an index card. Create a bowl full of rocks with a letter on each rock. Create a space where the child can use the card and rocks to build their name.	Index cards, Sharpie, rocks	Assessment photo
Cognitive Development Language Development Home Connection Fine Motor Development		**Morning Meeting:** 1. Good morning song (teacher's choice) 2. Monday: Morning Message **Letter/word focus:** O, o 3. Tues-Fri: **My News** - Talk with the students and write down one short sentence he/she says (i.e. "I like playing with my dog." —Joey)	Music device, whiteboard, chart paper, Sharpie, dry-erase marker	Assessment photo

STANDARDS	TIME	OUTDOOR ACTIVITIES	MATERIALS	DOCUMENTATION
Cognitive Development Language Development Gross Motor Development Sensory Development		Outdoor Time/Free Choice: *Optional activities include: watering plants, pulling weeds, gardening, sensory, snow painting, snowman building, snow shoveling, raking leaves, etc.*		Assessment photo
		Extra Activities:		

STANDARDS	TIME	LEARNING CENTER ACTIVITY CHOICES	MATERIALS	DOCUMENTATION
Cognitive Development Language Development Home Connection Fine Motor Development		WRITING: name, letter focus, My News. Use relevant writing sheets to complete writing time or allow the students time to freely draw and the teacher to dictate the students' drawings.	Highlighter, pencils, crayons	Assessment photo
Cognitive Development Sensory Development		SENSORY: Place sand, marbles, and golf tees in the sensory bin. Children try to set the marbles on the golf tees.	Sand, marbles, golf tees	Assessment photo
Cognitive Development Language Development Gross Motor Development Sensory Development Fine Motor Development		Learning Centers: *Note any changes and/or additions made to learning centers.*		Assessment photo

15

Cognitive Development Language Development Fine Motor Development Sensory Development		**Process Art:** Place a large piece of paper in an empty plastic baby pool. Then place small balls or marbles in cups of paint. Let children dip the balls in the paint, place in the pool, and work together to roll it around, creating a colorful piece of art.	Plastic baby pool, paint marbles or small balls, large paper	Assessment photo
Cognitive Development Language Development Fine Motor Development Sensory Development		**Question:** Why can't we float up to the sky? **View:** View a book with pictures of astronauts floating in space or use the Internet to provide a video of astronauts floating in space. **STEAM:** Place large paper on the ground, place pom-poms in watercolor paints. Help student stand on a chair, stool, or table (keep hands on the child the entire time for safety) and drop watercolor-soaked pom-poms on the paper for some splash art.	Large paper, pom-poms, watercolors/paint	Assessment photo

STANDARDS	TIME	CIRCLE TIME ACTIVITIES	MATERIALS	DOCUMENTATION
Cognitive Development Language Development Gross Motor Development		Circle Time: 1. Calendar activities (days, months, counting, number patterns, season, year) -Do squats while counting the days in the month. 2. Music & Movement:	Calendar, colored calendar numbers, music source	Assessment photo
Cognitive Development Language Development		Story Time: Books about gravity, space, astronauts, ramps, etc.		Assessment photo

STANDARDS	TIME	EXTRA ACTIVITIES	MATERIALS	DOCUMENTATION

2. Relevant Writing 1

Name Recognition and Practice

_____

Letter Recognition and Practice

O _____

o _____

2. Relevant Writing 2

*Write the student's news on the line below using a highlighter.

_____ •

*Encourage student to draw a picture of their news below.

2. Week 2 Shopping List

ITEMS	YES, we have this item	NO, we need to buy	$ COST of item	ITEMS	YES, we have this item	NO, we need to buy	$ COST of item
PROVOCATION: Index cards Sharpie rocks				SENSORY: Sand Marbles Golf tees			
MORNING MEETING: Music device Whiteboard chart paper Sharpie Dry erase marker				PROCESS ART: Baby pool Paint Marbles or small balls Large paper			
WRITING: Highlighter Chart paper Pencils				STEAM: Large paper Pom-poms Watercolors or paint			

2. Parent Letter

Dear Family,

This week your preschooler is learning about gravity! Talk to them at home about gravity and how it makes objects drop to the ground. Ask them what our lives would be like without gravity. They will perform art and engineering projects that demonstrate gravity. Oh, don't forget to ask them about their NEWS! They always have great things to tell their teachers.

Provocation: Name building with rocks	Sensory: Sand, golf tees, and marble stacking	Letter/Word Focus: O, o
Process Art: Baby pool, marble Art	STEM Project: Gravity	Writing: My News, letter O, o, name

DAILY SCHEDULE & PLANS

STANDARDS	TIME	ACTIVITY	MATERIALS	DOCUMENTATION
Cognitive Development Language Development	------	**Weekly Transition:** If your name starts with the letter ?, line up. *This transition should be used all week to move students from one activity/location to the next.*	Letters on index cards or something similar	
Cognitive Development	------	**Extension Center:** *What was successful and interesting to students last week? Carry this over to a center this week, so the students may extend this play/learning.*		
Cognitive Development		**Provocation:** Set out wood or cardboard frames along with nature pieces (rock, beads, nuts, leaves, sticks, etc.) for creating art pictures. Let the students take a picture of their creation.	Wood/cardboard frames, rocks, beads, nuts, etc.	
Parent Connection Cognitive Development Language Development Fine Motor Development		**Morning Meeting:** 1. Good morning song (teacher's choice) 2. Monday: Morning Message **Letter/word focus:** G, g/ Go 3. Tues–Fri: **My News**	Music device, whiteboard, chart paper, Sharpie, dry erase marker	

STANDARDS	TIME	ACTIVITY	MATERIALS	DOCUMENTATION
Cognitive Development Language Development Sensory Development		Outdoor Time/Free Choice: *Optional activities include: watering plants, pulling weeds, gardening, sensory, etc.*		Assessment photo
		Extra Activities:		
Cognitive Development Language Development Home Connection Fine Motor Development		Writing: name, letter focus, My News. Use relevant writing sheets to complete writing time or allow the students time to draw freely and the teacher to dictate the students' drawings.	Highlighter, pencils, crayons	Assessment photo
Cognitive Development Sensory Development		Sensory: Place lots of leaves and pine needles in the sensory bin for crunching and/or exploring. Add little animals or bugs, tweezers/tongs and bowls. Ask the children to find the bugs, pick them up with the tongs, and place them in the bowl. Then the student can count the bugs.	Leaves, pine needles, pine cones, plastic bugs, tweezers/tongs, bowls	Assessment photo
Cognitive Development Language Development Gross Motor Development Fine Motor Development Sensory Development		Learning Centers: *Note any changes and/or additions made to learning centers.*		Assessment photo
Cognitive Development		Process Art: Set out leaves, fall watercolors, paintbrushes, glue, and white/manila construction paper. Let the	Leaves, watercolors, paintbrushes, glue, white construction paper, Sharpie	Assessment photo

Language Development Sensory Development Fine Motor Development		students create. Ask them how their art makes them feel and dictate on or below piece.		
Cognitive Development Language Development Sensory Development Fine Motor Development		**Question:** Show students a tree and ask them about the parts of the tree. Trunk? Branches? Leaves? What does each part do? **View:** Use the Internet to view trees in a variety of weather conditions: rain, storm, wind, sunshine. **STEM/STEAM Project:** Provide the students with a variety of leaves, a paper towel roll (Make a 4–5-inch cut every half inch at the top of the roll and bend outward to create branches), glue, and a paintbrush for the glue. Ask the students to build a tree with a trunk, branches, and leaves. They can adjust the branches and glue on the leaves.	Leaves, paper towel rolls, glue, paintbrushes	Assessment photo
Cognitive Development Language Development Gross Motor Development		**Circle Time:** 1. Calendar activity (days, months, counting, number patterns, season, year) -Have the students tap their head while counting the days of the month. 2. Music & Movement:	Calendar, colored calendar numbers, music source	Assessment photo
Cognitive Development Language Development		**Story Time:** books related to clouds, water cycle, water, weather, and rain.		Assessment photo

3. Relevant Writing 1

*Write with a highlighter so child can trace if needed.

Name Recognition and Practice

_____

Letter Recognition and Practice

G_____

g_____

Go _____

25

3. Relevant Writing 2

*Write the student's news on the line below using a highlighter.

_____ •

*Encourage student to draw a picture of their news below.

3. Week 3 Shopping List

ITEMS	YES, we have this item	NO, we need to buy	$ COST Of item	ITEMS	YES, we have this item	NO, we need to buy	$ COST Of item
PROVOCATION: Wood/cardboard frames Rocks, beads, nuts, etc.				**SENSORY:** Leaves pine needles pine cones plastic bugs tweezers/tongs bowls			
MORNING MEETING: Music device Whiteboard Chart paper sharpie dry-erase marker				**PROCESS ART:** Leaves Watercolors paintbrushes glue			
				White construction paper Sharpie			
WRITING: Highlighter Chart paper Pencils				**STEAM:** Leaves Paper towel rolls Glue Paintbrushes			

3. Parent Letter

Dear Family,

This week your child will discuss the parts of a tree as well as exploring leaves, pine needles, and other natural objects. This is a great week to go on a nature walk with your child and help them to search for an object in nature (acorn, rock, leaf, etc.) to bring to class and share!

Provocation: Nature frames	Sensory: The Forest	Letter/Word Focus: G, g/Go
Process Art: Fall painting	STEM Project: Build a Tree	Writing: My News, letter G, g, Go, name

Thank you!

I want to sincerely thank you for purchasing Preschool Lesson Plans! I hope the experiences provided in each plan have allowed you to have fun and discover new things with your child or your class.

If you are enjoying Preschool Lesson Plans I would be grateful for you to write an Amazon review about your positive experience. Thank you!

Best,

Jessica

DAILY SCHEDULE & PLANS

STANDARDS	TIME	ACTIVITY	MATERIALS	DOCUMENTATION
Cognitive Development Language Development	------	**Weekly Transition:** If you are a boy/girl, line up.		
				Assessment
	------	**Extension Center:**		
Cognitive Development				Assessment photo
Cognitive Development		*What was successful and interesting to students last week? Carry this over to a center this week, so the students may extend this play/learning.* **Provocation:** Exploring graduating shades of blue. Place several bowls of paint from light blue to dark blue on a table along with blue paint swatches and blue items for inspiration. Let them explore and create freely with the colors on white construction paper.	White construction paper, blue paint swatches, blue items, blue, white paints, bowls, paintbrushes	Assessment Photo
Cognitive Development Language Development Home Connection Fine Motor Development		**Morning Meeting:** 1. Good morning song (teacher's choice) 2. Monday: Morning Message **Letter/word focus:** C, c / Dog 3. Tues-Fri: **My News** or use the word focus as a prompt (i.e., What do you know about dogs?)	Music device, whiteboard, chart paper, Sharpie, dry erase marker	Assessment photo

STANDARDS	TIME	ACTIVITY	MATERIALS	DOCUMENTATION
Cognitive Development Language Development Sensory Development		Outdoor Time/Free Choice: *Optional activities include: watering plants, pulling weeds, gardening, sensory, etc.* **Extra Activities:**		Assessment photo

STANDARDS	TIME	LEARNING CENTER ACTIVITY CHOICES	MATERIALS	DOCUMENTATION
Cognitive Development Language Development Home Connection Fine Motor Development		**Writing:** name, letter focus, My News. Use relevant writing sheets to complete writing time or allow the students time to freely draw and the teacher to dictate the students' drawings.	Highlighter, pencils, crayons	Assessment photo
Cognitive Development Sensory Development		**Sensory:** Fill the sensory bin with water, add plastic cups with holes in the bottom to simulate rain, and measuring cups. You can add boats or sea animals, too.	Water, plastic cups, boats, sea animals	Assessment photo
Cognitive Development Language Development Gross Motor Development Fine Motor Development Sensory Development		**Learning Centers:** *Note any changes and/or additions made to learning centers.*		Assessment photo
Cognitive Development Language Development Sensory Development Fine Motor Development		**Process Art:** Rain down art. Hang paper on a wire, fence, or wall. Provide water colors and pipettes, paintbrush or something that will provide a dripping technique. Let children dip the pipette into the watercolors and start dripping it from the top down. Dictate students' description onto the art or a separate piece of paper.	Construction paper, water colors, pipettes	Assessment photo
		Question: Where does the rain come from?	Clear jar, water, shaving cream, blue food coloring	Assessment photo

Cognitive Development
Language Development
Sensory Development
Fine Motor Development

View: Use the Internet to view clouds and rain. You may also view clips of the water cycle.

STEM/STEAM Project: Rain in a jar/cup.
Each student can have their own jar, or you can have a jar per group of students. Students fill jar almost to the top with water, then cover the top with shaving cream. Now, let the students drop blue food coloring on top of the shaving cream and wait for the blue to rain down into the water. This simulates exactly how a cloud works. Cloud fills with water and then rains/snows down.

STANDARDS	TIME	ACTIVITY	MATERIALS	DOCUMENTATION
Cognitive Development Language Development Gross Motor Development		**Circle Time:** **1.** Calendar activity (days, months, counting, number patterns, season, year) -Stomp while counting the days of the month.	Calendar, colored calendar numbers, music source	Assessment photo
Cognitive Development Language Development		**2.** Music & Movement: **Story Time:** Books related to clouds, water cycle, water, weather, and rain.		Assessment photo

4. Relevant Writing 1

*Write with a highlighter so child can trace if needed.

Name Recognition and Practice

_____

Letter Recognition and Practice

C_____

c_____

Dog_____

4. Relevant Writing 2

*Write the student's news on the line below using a highlighter.

•

*Encourage student to draw a picture of their news below.

4. Week 4 Shopping List

ITEMS	YES, we have this item	NO, we need to buy	$ COST Of item	ITEMS	YES, we have this item	NO, we need to buy	$ COST Of item
PROVOCATION: White construction paper Blue paint Swatches				WRITING: Highlighter chart Paper Pencils			
Blue items Blue paint White paints Bowls Paintbrushes				SENSORY: Water Plastic cups Boats			
MORNING MEETING: Music device Whiteboard Chart paper Sharpie Dry erase marker				PROCESS ART: Construction paper			
				Watercolors Pipettes			
				STEAM: Clear jar Water Shaving cream Blue food coloring			

4. Parent Letter

Dear Family,

This week your child will be learning about clouds, rain, and the water cycle. This will allow for great discussions at home along with the chance to do some serious cloud watching! Please bring your child a jar with a top for their "Rain in a Jar" experiment. If we do not have enough jars, then we will do the experiment in small groups.

Provocation: Exploring shades of blue	Sensory: Water and rain cups	Letter/Word Focus: C, c/Dog
Process Art: Dripping Watercolors	STEM Project: Water cycle	Writing: My News, letter C, c/Dog, name

DAILY SCHEDULE & PLANS

STANDARDS	TIME	DAILY ACTIVITIES	MATERIALS	DOCUMENTATION
Cognitive Development Language Development	------	Weekly Transition: introducing syllables. Clap each child's name and ask them how many claps are in their name. Slowly change the word "clap" to "syllables."		Assessment
Cognitive Development	------	Extension Center:		Assessment photo
Cognitive Development		*What was successful and interesting to students last week? Carry this over to a center this week, so the students may extend this play/learning.* Provocation: What can you make with wire? Place different lengths and colors of wire on a table along with some pictures of objects or books for inspiration. Allow children the freedom to explore and	Wire, books and pictures of objects for inspiration	Assessment photo

STANDARDS	TIME		MATERIALS	DOCUMENTATION
		create.		
Cognitive Development Language Development Home Connection Fine Motor Development		**Morning Meeting:** 1. Good morning song (teacher's choice) 2. Monday: Morning Message **Letter/word focus:** A, a/Dad 3. Tues-Fri: **My News writing prompt** *My dad … or Granddad …*	Music device, whiteboard, chart paper, Sharpie, Dry erase marker	Assessment photo

STANDARDS	TIME	OUTDOOR ACTIVITIES	MATERIALS	DOCUMENTATION
Cognitive Development Language Development Gross Motor Development Sensory Development		**Outdoor Time/Free Choice:** *Optional activities include: watering plants, pulling weeds, gardening, sensory, etc.* **Extra Activities:**		Assessment photo Assessment photo

STANDARDS	TIME	LEARNING CENTER ACTIVITY CHOICES	MATERIALS	DOCUMENTATION
Cognitive Development Language Development Home Connection Fine Motor Development		**WRITING:** name, letter focus, writing prompt/My News. Use relevant writing sheets to complete writing time or allow the students time to freely draw and the teacher to dictate the students' drawings.	Highlighter, pencils, or crayons	Assessment photo
Cognitive Development Sensory Development		**SENSORY:** Fill the bin with aluminum foil pieces for students to explore and create.	Aluminum foil	Assessment photo

	Learning Centers		Assessment photo
Cognitive Development Language Development Fine Motor Development Sensory Development Gross Motor Development			
	Note any changes and/or additions made to learning centers.		
Cognitive Development Language Development Sensory Development Fine Motor Development	**PROCESS ART:** Marble painting - Cut paper into interesting shapes. Create a box or tub where students can place paper. Students can dip marbles into paint using a spoon. Place the marble onto their construction paper and roll around to create a beautiful piece of art.	Marbles, shoe box/bin, paint, spoon, construction paper	Assessment photo
Cognitive Development Language Development Sensory Development Fine Motor Development	**Questions:** How does a roller coaster make you feel? What shapes do you see when you look at a roller coaster design?	Copy paper, pencils. blocks, PVC pipe or cardboard, paper towel rolls, cars, balls, marbles, cardstock, paper strips, glue	Assessment photo

View:
Let children watch a YouTube video of people riding roller coasters. Discuss what the person is feeling and the design of the coaster.

STEAM: Provide children with printed pictures of roller coasters. Give children copy paper and pencils. Ask them to draw their own roller coaster design.

STANDARDS	TIME	CIRCLE TIME ACTIVITIES	MATERIALS	DOCUMENTATION
Cognitive Development Language Development Gross Motor Development		**CIRCLE TIME:** **1.** Calendar activity (days, months, patterns, season, year). -Do sit-ups while counting the days of the month.	Calendar, colored calendar numbers, music source	Assessment photo
Cognitive Development Language Development		**2.** Music & Movement: **Story Time:** Books related to apples, fall, and amusement park brochures		Assessment photo

STANDARDS	TIME	EXTRA ACTIVITIES	MATERIALS	DOCUMENTATION

5. Relevant Writing 1

Name Recognition and Practice

_____

Letter Recognition and Practice

A_____

a _____

Dad_____

5. Relevant Writing 2

*Write the student's news on the line below using a highlighter.

_____ •

*Encourage student to draw a picture of their news below.

5. Week 5 Shopping List

ITEMS	YES, we have this item	NO, we need to buy	$ COST of item	ITEMS	YES, we have this item	NO, we need to buy	$ COST of item
PROVOCATION: Wire Book or pictures of objects for inspiration				PROCESS ART: Marbles Shoe box/bin Paint Spoon Construction paper			
MORNING MEETING: Music device White board Chart paper Sharpie Dry erase marker				STEAM: Copy paper Pencils Blocks PVC pipe or cardboard Paper towel rolls Cars Balls Marbles Cardstock Paper strips Glue			
WRITING: Highlighter Chart paper Pencils							
SENSORY: Aluminum foil							

5. Parent Letter

Dear Family,

This week your child will be discussing physics! We will talk about roller coasters and ramps. We will also build roller coasters and ramps, so we need your help. Please send a paper towel roll and/or a piece of cardboard. We will also need shoe boxes if you have any. Thank you!

Provocation: What can you make with wire?	Sensory: Explore aluminum foil!	Letter/Word Focus: A, a & Dad
Process Art: Marble painting	STEM Project: Roller coasters & ramps!	Writing: My News, letter A, a/ Dad name

DATE: _____   WEEK #: _6_   TITLE: _Roller Coasters 2_   TEACHER: _____

DAILY SCHEDULE & PLANS

STANDARDS	TIME	DAILY ACTIVITIES	MATERIALS	DOCUMENTATION
Cognitive Development Language Development	------	**Weekly Transition:** Rhyming (i.e., Will the person whose name rhymes with "Goosey" please line up. Lucy!)		Assessment
Cognitive Development	------	**Extension Center:**		Assessment photo
Cognitive Development		*What was successful and interesting to students last week? Carry this over to a center this week so that the students may extend this play/learning.* **Provocation:** Apples on a plate: paper, pencils, & apple color paints/watercolors. Encourage students to identify and draw the shapes and colors they see.	Apples, paper, pencil, watercolors	Assessment photo
Cognitive Development Language Development Home Connection Fine Motor Development		**Morning Meeting:** 1. Good morning song (teacher's choice) 2. Monday: Morning Message **Letter/word Focus:** T t, it 3. Tues-Fri: "My News" or **Writing Prompt** *What is your favorite food? It is…..*	Music device, white-board, chart paper, Sharpie, dry-erase marker	Assessment photo

STANDARDS	TIME	OUTDOOR ACTIVITIES	MATERIALS	DOCUMENTATION
Cognitive Development Language Development Gross Motor Development Sensory Development		**Outdoor time/Free Choice:** *Optional activities include: watering plants, pulling weeds, gardening, sensory, snow painting, snowman building, snow shoveling, raking leaves, etc.* **Extra Activities:**	Watering cans, water	Assessment photo

STANDARDS	TIME	LEARNING CENTER ACTIVITY CHOICES	MATERIALS	DOCUMENTATION
Cognitive Development Language Development Home Connection Fine Motor Development		**WRITING:** name, letter focus, My News/Writing Prompt. Use relevant writing sheets to complete writing time or allow the students time to freely draw and the teacher to dictate the students' drawing. Teacher can use the dictation to encourage identification of letters and words along with independent writing.	Highlighter, pencils or crayons	**Assessment** photo
Cognitive Development Sensory Development		**SENSORY:** Oats, fake apples, cinnamon sticks, small cups/buckets, measuring spoons and cups.	Oats, cinnamon sticks, buckets, apples, measuring spoons & cups	**Assessment** photo
Cognitive Development Language Development Gross Motor Development Sensory Development Fine Motor Development		**Learning Centers:** *Note any changes and/or additions made to learning centers*		**Assessment** photo
Cognitive Development Language Development Sensory Development Fine Motor Development		**PROCESS ART:** Make your own apple. Place apple cut-outs, glue, apple-color crayons, watercolors/paint, & tissue paper on the table. Provide real apples in a bowl or on a plate for the students to observe. Ask students to use the supplies to create their own apple.	Construction paper, glue, crayons, tissue paper, paint	**Assessment** photo
Cognitive Development Language Development Sensory Development		**Question:** How can you make a piece of paper stand up on its own? **View:** Review the roller coaster video. **Build Your Own Paper Coaster** Cut a piece of cardstock into 4 squares. Give each student a square and 11" x ½" strips of paper. The paper should be cut into different lengths and can even be creased or folded accordion style. Show the children how they can glue/tape each end down so that the paper will stand up in a 3-dimensional form.	Paper pieces, cardstock, glue, tape, stapler	**Assessment** photo

	Circle Time:	Calendar, colored calendar	Assessment
Cognitive Development	1. Calendar activities (days,	numbers, music source	Photo
Language Development	months, counting, number		
Gross Motor Development	patterns, season, year)		
	-Use a punching motion to		
	punch out the days of the		
	month.		
	2. Music & Movement:		
	Story Time:		Assessment
	Books related to apples, fall,		Photo
	and amusement park		
Cognitive Development	brochures		
Language Development			

STANDARDS	TIME	EXTRA ACTIVITIES	MATERIALS	DOCUMENTATION

6. Relevant Writing 1

Name Recognition and Practice

_____

Letter Recognition and Practice

T_____

t_____

It_____

6. Relevant Writing 2

*Write the student's news on the line below using a highlighter.

_____

*Encourage student to draw a picture of their news below.

6. Week 6 Shopping List

ITEMS	YES, we have this item	NO, we need to buy	$ COST of item	ITEMS	YES, we have this item	NO, we need to buy	$ COST of item
PROVOCATION: Apples Paper Pencil watercolors				SENSORY: Oats cinnamon sticks Buckets Apples Measuring spoons			
MORNING MEETING: Music device White board chart paper sharpie dry-erase marker				PROCESS ART: Construction paper Glue Crayons tissue paper Paint			
WRITING: Highlighter chart paper Pencils				STEAM: Paper pieces Cardstock Glue Tape staple			

6. Parent Letter

Dear Family,

This week your preschooler will continue exploring the world of Roller Coasters and Design. If you have a brochure from an amusement park please send with your child. They will also explore apples and still art.

Provocation: Apples on a plate: Shapes & still art	Sensory: Oats, apples, & cinnamon sticks	Letter/Word Focus: Tt, it
Process Art: Make your own apple. Choose your medium	STEM Project: 3D coaster designs	Writing: What is your favorite food? It is….

DAILY SCHEDULE & PLANS

STANDARDS	TIME	DAILY ACTIVITIES	MATERIALS	DOCUMENTATION
Language Development Cognitive Development	------	**Weekly Transition:** Name Recognition (Ask children to line up by showing a name on a name plate)	Name plates (Note card with students' first name)	Assessment
Cognitive Development	------	**Extension Center:**		Photo Assessment
Cognitive Development		*What was successful and interesting to students last week? Carry this over to a center this week, so the students may extend this play/learning.* **Provocation:** Leaf People: leaves, glue, eyes, twigs/cut paper & an example of a "leaf person". This activity can be extended by asking the student to tell about his/her leaf person and the teacher dictating the story.	Leaves, glue, eyes, paper	Photo Assessment
Language Development Cognitive Development Home Connection Fine Motor Development Social/Emotional Dev.		**Morning Meeting:** 1. Good morning song (Teacher's choice) 2. Monday: Morning Message **Letter/Word Focus:** Mm, cat 3. Tues-Fri: **"My News"/ Writing Prompt** *Tell me about cats. Cats….*	Music device, white-board, chart paper, sharpie, dry-erase marker	Photo Assessment

STANDARDS	TIME	OUTDOOR ACTIVITIES	MATERIALS	DOCUMENTATION
Social/Emotional Dev. Language Development Cognitive Development Sensory Development Gross Motor Development		**Outdoor time/Free Choice:**	Watering cans, water	Photo Assessment
		Optional activities include: watering plants, pulling weeds, gardening, sensory, snow painting, snowman building, snow shoveling, raking leaves, etc. **Extra Activities:**		

STANDARDS	TIME	LEARNING CENTER ACTIVITY CHOICES	MATERIALS	DOCUMENTATION
Language Development Cognitive Development Home Connection Fine Motor Development		**WRITING:** Name, Letter Focus, My News/Writing Prompt. Use relevant writing sheets to complete writing time or allow the students time to freely draw and the teacher to dictate the students' drawing. Teacher can use the dictation to encourage identification of letters and words along with independent writing.	Highlighter, pencils or crayons	Photo Assessment
Cognitive Development Sensory Development		**SENSORY:** Water, googly eyes, measuring spoons, cups, and tweezers to pick up googly eyes.	Water, googly eyes, measuring spoons, cups, tweezers	Photo Assessment
Language Development Cognitive Development Fine Motor Development Gross Motor Social/Emotional Dev.		**Learning Centers:** *Note any changes and/or additions made to learning centers*		Photo Assessment
Language Development Cognitive Development Sensory Development Fine Motor Development		**PROCESS ART:** Black & Orange Inspired Art. This can include construction paper pieces, orange & black crayons, paint, and/or markers. There should be a variety of materials so each student can create their own, unique piece of art.	Black and orange items for collaging & glue	Photo Assessment
Language Development Cognitive Development Sensory Development Fine Motor Development Social/Emotional Dev.		**Question:** What is inside a pumpkin? **View:** Use a video or a book to view a pumpkin growing and/or someone making pumpkin pie. **STEM:** Explore the Pumpkin Guts Dictate what the students think is inside the pumpkin & how it feels. Cut the top of the pumpkin and allow children to take turns digging out the pumpkin guts. Ask children to separate the seeds & save them for later projects. Ask questions about what they see, feel, and smell. How do we make pumpkin	Pumpkin Spoons Cups Paper towels	Photo Assessment

pie?

STANDARDS	TIME	CIRCLE TIME ACTIVITIES	MATERIALS	DOCUMENTATION
		CIRCLE TIME:	Calendar, colored calendar numbers, music source	Photo Assessment
Cognitive Development Language Development Gross Motor Development Social/Emotional Dev.		**1.** Calendar Activities (Days, Months, Counting, Number Patterns, Season, Year) -Hop on one foot while counting the days of the month		
Cognitive Development Language Development Social/Emotional Dev.		**2.** Music & Movement: **Story Time:** Books related to fall, October, Halloween, feeling scared, and pumpkins		Photo Assessment

STANDARDS	TIME	EXTRA ACTIVITIES	MATERIALS	DOCUMENTATION

7. Relevant Writing 1

Name Recognition and Practice

_____

Letter Recognition and Practice

M_____

m_____

Cat_____

7. Relevant Writing 2

*Write the student's news on the line below using a highlighter.

•

*Encourage student to draw a picture of their news below.

7. Week 7 Shopping List

ITEMS	YES, we have this item	NO, we need to buy	$ COST Of item	ITEMS	YES, we have this item	NO, we need to buy	$ COST Of item
PROVOCATION: Leaves Glue Eyes paper				SENSORY: Water googly eye Measuring spoons Cups tweezers			
MORNING MEETING: Music device White-board chart paper sharpie dry-erase marker				PROCESS ART: Black and orange items for collaging & glue			
WRITING: Highlighter chart paper Pencils				STEAM: Pumpkin Spoons Cups Paper towels			

7. Parent Letter

Dear Family,

This week your preschooler will explore the PUMPKIN! Please send a small pumpkin with your child for process art next week. We can't wait to see the variety of pumpkins that will be created! Be sure to ask your child about the leaf person he/she created this week.

Provocation: Leaf People Made from nature	Sensory: Water & Googly Eyes	Letter/Word Focus: Mm, Cat
Process Art: Black & Orange Collaging	STEM Project: Pumpkin Guts	Writing: Cats....

DAILY SCHEDULE & PLANS

STANDARDS	TIME	DAILY ACTIVITIES	MATERIALS	DOCUMENTATION
Cognitive Development Language Development	------	**Weekly Transition:** Colors (i.e. If you have the color red on please line up. Hold up color cards or crayons for visual recognition.)	Color cards or crayons	Assessment
Cognitive Development	------	**Extension Center:**		Assessment Photo
Cognitive Development		*What was successful and interesting to students last week? Carry this over to a center this week, so the students may extend this play/learning.* **Provocation:** Set out Q-tips, glue and black construction paper. Students can explore and create their own design.	Q-tips, black construction paper, glue	Assessment Photo
Cognitive Development Language Development Social/Emotional Dev. Fine Motor Development		**Morning Meeting:** 1. Good morning song (Teacher's choice) 2. Monday: Morning Message Letter/Word Focus: Ll, to 3. Tues-Fri: **"My News"**/ **Writing Prompt:** Where do you like to go? I go to...	Music device, white-board, chart paper, sharpie, dry-erase marker	Assessment Photo

STANDARDS	TIME	OUTDOOR ACTIVITIES	MATERIALS	DOCUMENTATION
Cognitive Development Language Development Gross Motor Development Sensory Development Social/Emotional Dev.		**Outdoor time/Free Choice:** *Optional activities include: watering plants, pulling weeds, gardening, sensory, snow painting, snowman building, snow shoveling, raking leaves, collecting rocks, etc.*		Assessment Photo
		Extra Activities:		

STANDARDS	TIME	LEARNING CENTER ACTIVITY CHOICES	MATERIALS	DOCUMENTATION
		WRITING: Name, Letter Focus, My News/Writing	Highlighter, pencils or crayons	Assessment Photo

Cognitive Development Language Development Fine Motor Development	Prompt. Use relevant writing sheets to complete writing time or allow the students time to freely draw and the teacher to dictate the students' drawing. Teacher can use the dictation to encourage identification of letters and words along with independent writing.	
Cognitive Development Sensory Development	**SENSORY:** Pretend spiders, rice, tweezers and jars. Challenge the students to use the tweezers to pick up the pretend spiders and fill the jars. Which jar has more or less?	Spider/spider rings, rice, tweezers, jars — Assessment Photo
Cognitive Development Language Development Gross Motor Development Sensory Development Social/Emotional Dev. Fine Motor Development	**Learning Centers:** *Note any changes and/or additions made to learning centers*	Assessment Photo
Cognitive Development Language Development Sensory Development Fine Motor Development	**PROCESS ART:** Small Pumpkin Decorating. Prepare the table with paint, sharpies, glue, glitter, and googly eyes. Supervise the students while they decorate their very own pumpkin.	Paint, Sharpies (With supervision), glue, googly eyes, and glitter — Assessment Photo
Cognitive Development Language Development Sensory Development Social/Emotional Dev. Fine Motor Development	**Question:** Why doesn't a tall building fall over? **View:** Show students picture of buildings, bridges and other structures that are being built or already built. Talk about the shapes you see that hold the structure up and keep it from falling. **STEM/STEAM:** Candy Pumpkin Toothpick Build: Then provide students with gummy pumpkin and toothpicks. Demonstrate how triangles help to hold a structure up. Let the children experiment with their own building.	Gummy pumpkin/ marshmallows, toothpicks — Assessment Photo

STANDARDS	TIME	CIRCLE TIME ACTIVITIES	MATERIALS	DOCUMENTATION
Cognitive Development Language Development Gross Motor Development Social/Emotional Dev.		**CIRCLE TIME:** **1.** Calendar Activities (Days, Months, Counting, Number Patterns, Season, Year) -Bend over and touch your toes while counting the days of the month	Calendar, colored calendar numbers, music source	**Assessment** **Photo**
		2. Music & Movement:		
Cognitive Development Language Development Social/Emotional Dev.		**Story Time:** Books about skyscrapers, bridges, construction, fall, pumpkins, Halloween		**Assessment** **Photo**

STANDARDS	TIME	EXTRA ACTIVITIES	MATERIALS	DOCUMENTATION

8. Relevant Writing 1

Name Recognition and Practice

_____

Letter Recognition and Practice

L_____

I_____

To_____

8. Relevant Writing 2

*Write the student's news on the line below using a highlighter.

_____

*Encourage student to draw a picture of their news below.

8. Week 8 Shopping List

ITEMS	YES, we have this item	NO, we need to buy	$ COST Of item	ITEMS	YES, we have this item	NO, we need to buy	$ COST Of item
PROVOCATION: Q-tips black construction paper glue **MORNING MEETING:** Music device White-board chart paper sharpie dry-erase marker **WRITING:** Highlighter chart paper Pencils				SENSORY: Spider/ spider rings Rice Tweezers Jars **PROCESS ART:** Paint Sharpies Glue glitter **STEAM:** Gummy pumpkin/ marshmallows toothpicks			

8. Parent Letter

Dear Family,

This week your preschooler will explore ENGINEERING! Students will observe skyscrapers, bridges, and other structures. They will identify shapes such as triangles, squares, etc. to determine what the structure needs to stand strong. Students will try out their engineering skills by building with gummy pumpkins and toothpicks. We should have some very unique structures!

Provocation: Q-Tip Designs	**Sensory:** Spider/Rice Find	**Letter/Word Focus:** Ll, to
Process Art: Pumpkin Decorating	**STEM Project:** Candy Pumpkin Toothpick Engineering	**Writing:** I go to...

DAILY SCHEDULE & PLANS

STANDARDS	TIME	DAILY ACTIVITIES	MATERIALS	DOCUMENTATION
Cognitive Development Language Development	------	**Weekly Transition:** Name Recognition. Hold up an index card with a student's name on it. Have the student transition when he sees his name.	Name Cards or Names printed on an index card	Assessment
Cognitive Development	------	**Extension Center:**		Assessment Photo
Cognitive Development		*What was successful and interesting to students last week? Carry this over to a center this week, so the students may extend this play/learning.* **Provocation:** Fall Leaf collages. Prepare the table with a variety of leaves. Allow the students to glue the leaves onto a piece of construction paper or cardstock and create their own collage. You may also provide scissors for students to cut the leaves into different shapes and sizes.	Leaves, glue, construction paper, scissors	Assessment Photo
Cognitive Development Language Development Social/Emotional Dev. Fine Motor Development		**Morning Meeting:** 1. Good morning song (Teacher's choice) 2. Monday: Morning Message **Letter/Word Focus:** Uu, My 3. Tues-Fri: **"My News"** **/Writing Prompt:** What is your favorite color? My favorite color is.....	Music device, white-board, chart paper, sharpie, dry-erase marker	Assessment Photo

STANDARDS	TIME	OUTDOOR ACTIVITIES	MATERIALS	DOCUMENTATION
Cognitive Development Language Development Gross Motor Development Sensory Development Social/Emotional Dev.		**Outdoor time/Free Choice:** *Optional activities include: watering plants, pulling weeds, gardening, sensory, snow painting, snowman building, snow shoveling, raking leaves, collecting rocks, etc.*		Assessment Photo
		Extra Activities:		

STANDARDS	TIME	LEARNING CENTER ACTIVITY CHOICES	MATERIALS	DOCUMENTATION
Cognitive Development Language Development Fine Motor Development		**WRITING:** Name, Letter Focus, My News/Writing Prompt. Use relevant writing sheets to complete writing time or allow the students time to freely draw and the teacher to dictate the students' drawing. Teacher can use the dictation to encourage identification of letters and words along with independent writing.	Highlighter, pencils or crayons	Assessment Photo
Cognitive Development Sensory Development		**SENSORY:** Leaves, acorns, and previously learned letters (these can be cut out or magnet letters). Provide tweezers and cups. Students can go on a letter hunt.	Letters, leaves, acorns	Assessment Photo
Cognitive Development Language Development Gross Motor Development Sensory Development Social/Emotional Dev. Fine Motor Development		**Learning Centers:** *Note any changes and/or additions made to learning centers*		Assessment Photo
Cognitive Development Language Development Sensory Development Fine Motor Development		**PROCESS ART:** Foil printed fall trees. Talk about the size and shape of a tree trunk. Provide students the materials to draw a tree trunk. Use foil to dip into fall colors and allow students the freedom to create their own tree tops.	Aluminum foil, fall paint colors, construction paper, brown crayons/pastels for tree trunks	Assessment Photo
Cognitive Development Language Development Sensory Development Social/Emotional Dev. Fine Motor Development		**Question:** Give each child a leaf and ask them what they see on the leaf. **View:** View a leaf changing from summer, fall, winter, spring via media or a book.	Leaves, media source, crayons, paper, Sharpies	Assessment Photo

STEM/STEAM PROJECT:
Explore a leaf, discuss the
color & veins, Show children
how to do leaf rubbings
and/or use a Sharpie to
directly follow the veins in
the leaf. They may also use
Sharpies to color in the
negative space between the
veins of the leaf for an art
piece.

STANDARDS	TIME	CIRCLE TIME ACTIVITIES	MATERIALS	DOCUMENTATION
Cognitive Development Language Development Gross Motor Development Social/Emotional Dev.		**CIRCLE TIME:** 1. Calendar Activities (Days, Months, Counting, Number Patterns, Season, Year) -do jumping jacks while counting the days of the month	Calendar, colored calendar numbers, music source	Assessment Photo
		2. Music & Movement:		
Cognitive Development Language Development Social/Emotional Dev.		**Story Time:** Books about fall, trees, leaves, harvest, Thanksgiving		Assessment Photo

STANDARDS	TIME	EXTRA ACTIVITIES	MATERIALS	DOCUMENTATION

9. Relevant Writing 1

*Write with a highlighter so child can trace if needed.

Name Recognition and Practice

_____

Letter Recognition and Practice

U_____

u_____

my_____

9. Relevant Writing 2

*Write the student's news on the line below using a highlighter.

---

*Encourage student to draw a picture of their news below.

9. Week 9 Shopping List

ITEMS	YES, we have this item	NO, we need to buy	$ COST Of item	ITEMS	YES, we have this item	NO, we need to buy	$ COST Of item
PROVOCATION: Leaves Glue construction paper Scissors				SENSORY: Letters Leaves acorns			
MORNING MEETING: Music device White-board chart paper sharpie dry-erase marker				PROCESS ART: Paint Sharpies Glue googly eye glitter			
WRITING: Highlighter chart paper Pencils				STEAM: Leaves media source Crayons Paper Sharpies			

9. Parent Letter

Dear Family,

This week your child will explore the parts of a leaf and understand why leaves change colors. They will view the leaf process from spring to winter and then use real leaves to explore, discuss, and create art from nature.

Provocation: Leaf animals/people	Sensory: Fall letter search Leaves, acorns, and previously learned letters	Letter/Word Focus: U, My
Process Art: Foil printing	STEM Project: Why leaves change and leaf veins	Writing: My favorite color...

DAILY SCHEDULE & PLANS

STANDARDS	TIME	DAILY ACTIVITIES	MATERIALS	DOCUMENTATION
Cognitive Development Language Development	------	**Weekly Transition:** Clapping Syllables of students' names. Clap the syllables while stating the name and ask the student to repeat it.		Assessment
Cognitive Development	------	**Extension Center:**		Assessment Photo
Cognitive Development		*What was successful and interesting to students last week? Carry this over to a center this week, so the students may extend this play/learning.* **Provocation:** Rulers, markers, pencils and big paper. Show the students how to use a ruler to draw lines. Then let them explore with the lines and designs on a large sheet of paper.	Rulers, markers, pencils, big paper	Assessment Photo
Cognitive Development Language Development Social/Emotional Dev. Fine Motor Development		**Morning Meeting:** 1. Good morning song (Teacher's choice) 2. Monday: Morning Message **Letter/Word Focus:** Ee, Mom 3. Tues-Fri: **"My News"/** **Writing Prompt:** Tell me about your mom. My mom…..	Music device, white-board, chart paper, sharpie, dry-erase marker	Assessment Photo

STANDARDS	TIME	OUTDOOR ACTIVITIES	MATERIALS	DOCUMENTATION
Cognitive Development Language Development Gross Motor Development Sensory Development Social/Emotional Dev.		Outdoor time/Free Choice: *Optional activities include: watering plants, pulling weeds, gardening, sensory, snow*		Assessment Photo

painting, snowman building,
snow shoveling, raking leaves,
collecting rocks, etc.

Extra Activities:

STANDARDS	TIME	LEARNING CENTER ACTIVITY CHOICES	MATERIALS	DOCUMENTATION
		WRITING: Name, Letter Focus, My News/Writing Prompt. Use relevant writing sheets to complete writing time or allow the students time to freely draw and the teacher to dictate the students' drawing. Teacher can use the dictation to encourage identification of letters and words along with independent writing.	Highlighter, pencils or crayons	Assessment Photo
Cognitive Development Language Development Fine Motor Development				
Cognitive Development Sensory Development		**SENSORY:** Pumpkin seed, fine motor play. Place pumpkin seeds, small pumpkins (real/toy) and some leaves (real/pretend) into the sensory bin along with tweezers and a bowl. Ask the children to see how many pumpkin seeds they can place in the bowl using the tongs. Practice counting and comparing the bowls using the words "more" and "less""	Pumpkin seeds, pumpkins, leaves, tweezers, bowls	Assessment Photo
Cognitive Development Language Development Gross Motor Development Sensory Development Social/Emotional Dev. Fine Motor Development		**Learning Centers:** *Note any changes and/or additions made to learning center*		Assessment Photo
Cognitive Development		**PROCESS ART:** Tape Resist process art. Cut a variety of lengths of painter's tape. Let the children design the tape	Painter's tape, cardstock, watercolors, paint brushes	Assessment Photo

77

Language Development Sensory Development Fine Motor Development		pieces onto a sheet of cardstock. Provide a variety of watercolors for the student to paint. After the paint dries remove the painter's tape. The tape should remove easily and reveal the art piece.		
Cognitive Development Language Development Sensory Development Social/Emotional Dev. Fine Motor Development		**Question:** Who was at the first Thanksgiving? What type of home did the Native Americans live in?	Paper plate (big or small), paint, paint brushes,	**Assessment Photo**
		View: View images and/or videos of real Native American Teepees.		
		STEM/STEAM PROJECT: Build a Teepee! Cut a paper plate in ½ and allow the children to decorate one side of the plate. Fold the paper plate into a cone shape (teepee) and staple to create a 3-D art piece.		

STANDARDS	TIME	CIRCLE TIME ACTIVITIES	MATERIALS	DOCUMENTATION
Cognitive Development Language Development Gross Motor Development Social/Emotional Dev.		**CIRCLE TIME:** 1. Calendar Activities (Days, Months, Counting, Patterns, Season, Year) - jump while counting the days of the month.	Calendar, colored calendar numbers, music source	**Assessment Photo**
		2. Music & Movement:		
Cognitive Development Language Development Social/Emotional Dev.		**Story Time:** Books about fall, trees, leaves, plant, Thanksgiving, Native Americans		**Assessment Photo**

10. Relevant Writing 1

*Write with a highlighter so child can trace if needed.

Name Recognition and Practice

_____

Letter Recognition and Practice

E_____

e_____

Mom_____

10. Relevant Writing 2

*Write the student's news on the line below using a highlighter.

*Encourage student to draw a picture of their news below.

10. Week 10 Shopping List

ITEMS	YES, we have this item	NO, we need to buy	$ COST Of item	ITEMS	YES, we have this item	NO, we need to buy	$ COST Of item
PROVOCATION: Rulers Markers Pencils big paper				**SENSORY:** Pumpkin seeds pumpkins leaves tweezers bowls			
MORNING MEETING: Music device White-board chart paper sharpie dry-erase marker				**PROCESS ART:** Painter's tape cardstock Watercolors paint brushes			
WRITING: Highlighter paper Pencils				**STEAM:** Paper plate (big or small) Paint paint brushes			

10. Parent Letter

Dear Family,

Let's begin our road toward Thanksgiving! This time of the year provides so many teachable moments. This week we will begin discussing the First Thanksgiving. You can discuss with your child what Thanksgiving means to your family.

Provocation:	Sensory:	Letter/Word Focus:
Straight line art with rulers	Pumpkin seed find and count	E,e
Process Art:	**STEM Project:**	**Writing:**
Tape Resist process art	Build a Teepee!	My mom...

DATE _____ WEEK #: _11_ TITLE: __Clay Dishes__ TEACHER: _____

Daily Schedule & Plans

STANDARDS	TIME	DAILY ACTIVITIES	MATERIALS	DOCUMENTATION
Cognitive Development Language Development	------	**Weekly Transition:** Name the shape. Simply place a variety of shapes in your pocket. Ask each student to name the shape you pull out in order to line up.	Shape cut-outs or Tangrams of different shapes	
Cognitive Development	------	**Extension Center:**		
Cognitive Development		*What was successful and interesting to students last week? Carry this over to a center this week, so the students may extend this play/learning.* **Provocation:** Decorate a Turkey. Provide a Turkey cut-out of construction paper along with water colors/markers/paint/crayons, feathers, and glue for students to create their own unique turkey. If students come on multiple days then have watercolors on Monday, crayons on Tues, feathers to glue on Wed, and googly eyes on Thurs/Friday.	Turkey cut-out of construction paper, watercolors, crayons, feathers, glue, googly eyes, paintbrushes	
Cognitive Development Language Development Home Connection Fine Motor Development		**Morning Meeting:** 1. Good morning song (Teacher's choice) 2. Monday: Morning Message **Letter/Word Focus:** Ii, I 3. Tues-Fri: **"My News"** Writing Prompt: What are you thankful for? I am thankful for….	Music device, white-board, chart paper, sharpie, dry-erase marker	

STANDARDS	TIME	OUTDOOR ACTIVITIES	MATERIALS	DOCUMENTATION
Cognitive Development Language Development Gross Motor Development Sensory Development		**Outdoor time/Free Choice:** *Optional activities include: watering plants, pulling weeds, gardening, sensory, snow painting, snowman building, snow shoveling, raking leaves, etc.* **Extra Activities:**		

STANDARDS	TIME	LEARNING CENTER	MATERIALS	DOCUMENTATION

Cognitive Development Language Development Home Connection Fine Motor Development	**WRITING:** Name, Letter Focus, My News/Writing Prompt. Use relevant writing sheets to complete writing time or allow the students time to freely draw and the teacher to dictate the students' drawing. Teacher can use the dictation to encourage identification of letters and words along with independent writing.	Highlighter, pencils or crayons
Cognitive Development Sensory Development	**SENSORY:** Corn shucking. Provide students with dried corn on the cobs and/or Indian corn and allow them to shuck and pull the kernels off into the sensory bin.	Dried Corn, Indian Corn on the Cob
Cognitive Development Language Development Gross Motor Development Sensory Development Fine Motor Development	**Learning Centers:** *Note any changes and/or additions made to learning centers*	
Cognitive Development Language Development Sensory Development Fine Motor Development	**PROCESS ART:** Pumpkin Seed Dying. Use the pumpkin seeds from last week. Students will place seeds in a small plastic sandwich bag, choose a watercolor and squirt in the bag, move the seeds around until they are completely covered, then set on a paper towel to dry. Students are given a small square piece of cardstock to create their own colorful art piece from the dyed pumpkin seeds.	Pumpkin seeds, plastic sandwich bag, bags, watercolors, square pieces of cardstock
Cognitive Development Language Development Sensory Development	**Question:** What did Native Americans drink from and eat on? Do you think their dishes look like ours? Where did their dishes come from?	Clay or air-dry clay, water
	View: View Native Americans creating dishware out of clay.	

85

STEM/STEAM PROJECT:
Native American Clay cup or plate. Show students how to wet the tips of their fingers to work and smooth the clay. Provide a demonstration of rolling a small piece of clay into a ball and then using your thumb to push down in the center of the ball to create space (like a cup) Students will and then begin molding their own clay cup or plate. You may also use air-dry clay.

STANDARDS	TIME	CIRCLE TIME ACTIVITIES	MATERIALS	DOCUMENTATION
Cognitive Development Language Development Gross Motor Development		**CIRCLE TIME:** **1.** Calendar Activities (Days, Months, Counting, Patterns, Season, Year) -Do push-ups while counting the days of the month	Calendar, colored calendar numbers, music source	
		2. Music & Movement:		
Cognitive Development Language Development		**Story Time:** Books about fall, trees, leaves, plant, Thanksgiving, Native Americans		

11. Relevant Writing 1

*Write with a highlighter so child can trace if needed.

Name Recognition and Practice

_____

Letter Recognition and Practice

I_____

i_____

I_____

11. Relevant Writing 2

*Write the student's news on the line below using a highlighter.

_____

*Encourage student to draw a picture of their news below.

11. Week 11 Shopping List

ITEMS	YES, we have this item	NO, we need to buy	$ COST Of item	ITEMS	YES, we have this item	NO, we need to buy	$ COST Of item
PROVOCATION: Turkey cut-out of construction paper				SENSORY: Dried Corn			
watercolors crayons Feathers Glue googly eyes paintbrushes				PROCESS ART: Pumpkin seeds plastic sandwich bags			
MORNING MEETING: Music device White-board chart paper sharpie dry-erase marker				watercolors square pieces of cardstock			
WRITING: Highlighter chart paper Pencils				STEAM: Clay or air-dry clay water			

11. Parent Letter

Dear Family,

Happy Thanksgiving! Discuss with your child all the things you are thankful for and then ask them what they are thankful for. You may be surprised at their answers! Also, please check out your child's Teepee this week. They will be every excited to show you their masterpiece.

Provocation: Decorate your own Turkey	Sensory: Corn shucking	Letter/Word Focus: I, i/ I
Process Art: Pumpkin Seed Dying	STEAM Project: Native American clay cups/plates	Writing: I am thankful for….

DAILY SCHEDULE & PLANS

STANDARDS	TIME	DAILY ACTIVITIES	MATERIALS	DOCUMENTATION
Language Development Cognitive Development	-------	**Weekly Transition:** Review of Letters. Have letters written on cards, stones, etc. Pull one out and ask student to name the letter. Use all the letters students have learned thus far.	Letter cards or stones	Assessment
Cognitive Development	------	**Extension Center:**		Assessment Photo
Cognitive Development		*What was successful and interesting to students last week? Carry this over to a center this week, so the students may extend this play/learning.* **Provocation:** Fall Wreath. Provide students with a paper plate (cut-out the middle to represent a wreath), glue and bowls of fall colors, textures, & materials to create their own Fall Wreath. This is a great time to gather all your excess fall materials and place them on the table for one last project!	Paper plate, glue, fall materials	Assessment Photo
Language Development Cognitive Development Home Connection Fine Motor Development Social/Emotional Dev.		**Morning Meeting:** 1. Good morning song (Teacher's choice) 2. Monday: Morning Message **Letter/Word Focus: Rr, are** 3. Tues-Fri: **"My News"/ Writing Prompt:** What are you doing for Thanksgiving? We are….	Music device, white-board, chart paper, sharpie, dry-erase marker	Assessment Photo

STANDARDS	TIME	OUTDOOR ACTIVITIES	MATERIALS	DOCUMENTATION
Social/Emotional Dev. Language Development Cognitive Development Sensory Development Gross Motor Development		**Outdoor time/Free Choice:** *Optional activities include: watering plants, pulling weeds, gardening, sensory, snow painting, snowman building, snow shoveling, raking leaves, etc.*		Assessment Photo

Extra Activities:

STANDARDS	TIME	LEARNING CENTER ACTIVITY CHOICES	MATERIALS	DOCUMENTATION
Language Development Cognitive Development Home Connection Fine Motor Development		WRITING: Name, Letter Focus, My News/Writing Prompt. Use relevant writing sheets to complete writing time or allow the students time to freely draw and the teacher to dictate the students' drawing. Teacher can use the dictation to encourage identification of letters and words along with independent writing.	Highlighter, pencils or crayons	Assessment Photo
Cognitive Development Sensory Development		SENSORY: Apple pie! Fill the sensory bin with oats, apples (fake/real), measuring spoons, and small pie tins for students to explore.	Apples (real/fake), oats, measuring spoons, pie tins	Assessment Photo
Language Development Cognitive Development Fine Motor Development Gross Motor Social/Emotional Dev.		Learning Centers: *Note any changes and/or additions made to learning centers		Assessment Photo
Language Development Cognitive Development Sensory Development Fine Motor Development		PROCESS ART: Native American Sand Painting. Using a tray for easy clean-up provide students with card stock, pencil, glue and sand. Students can draw their own designs and then apply glue to their design. They will cover the picture in sand, shake off excess sand and present their masterpiece!	Cardstock, glue, pencils.	Assessment Photo
Language Development Cognitive Development Sensory Development Fine Motor Development Social/Emotional Dev.		Questions: What did the Native Americans paint on their dishes?	Paint, paintbrushes	Assessment Photo
		View: View Native American dishware and discuss the		

93

colors and designs painted on
the dishes.

STEM/STEAM PROJECT:
Have students paint their clay
cups/plates using the Native
American influence.

STANDARDS	TIME	CIRCLE TIME ACTIVITIES	MATERIALS	DOCUMENTATION
Cognitive Development Language Development Gross Motor Development Social/Emotional Dev.		**CIRCLE TIME:** **1.** Calendar Activities (Days, Months, Counting, Patterns, Season, Year) -Stomp feet while counting the days of the month	Calendar, colored calendar numbers, music source	Assessment Photo
Cognitive Development Language Development Social/Emotional Dev.		**2.** Music & Movement: **Story Time:** Books about fall, trees, leaves, plant, Thanksgiving, Native Americans, food		Assessment Photo

STANDARDS	TIME	EXTRA ACTIVITIES	MATERIALS	DOCUMENTATION

12. Relevant Writing 1

*Write with a highlighter so child can trace if needed.

Name Recognition and Practice

_____

Letter Recognition and Practice

R_____

r_____

are

_____

12. Relevant Writing 2

*Write the student's news on the line below using a highlighter.

---

*Encourage student to draw a picture of their news below.

12. Week 12 Shopping List

ITEMS	YES, we have this item	NO, we need to buy	$ COST Of item	ITEMS	YES, we have this item	NO, we need to buy	$ COST Of item
PROVOCATION: Paper plate Glue fall materials				SENSORY: Apples (real/fake) oats measuring spoons pie tins			
MORNING MEETING: Music device White-board chart paper sharpie dry-erase marker				PROCESS ART: Cardstock Glue Pencils			
WRITING: Highlighter paper Pencils				STEAM: Paint paintbrushes			

12. Parent Letter

Dear Family,

We are in the Thanksgiving spirit! Your child has been learning about the First Thanksgiving and Native Americans. They will be finishing their Native American clay cups/plates this week. Be sure to take these home, so your child can share them with family over the holiday.

Provocation: Fall Wreath	Sensory: Apple pie	Letter/Word Focus: Rr, Are
Process Art: Native American Sand Painting	STEAM Project: Painting Clay cups/plates	Writing: What are you doing for Thanksgiving? We are _____.

DATE: _____ WEEK #: _13_ TITLE: __Kwanzaa__ TEACHER: _____

DAILY SCHEDULE & PLANS

STANDARDS	TIME	DAILY ACTIVITIES	MATERIALS	DOCUMENTATION
Language Development Cognitive Development	------	**Weekly Transition:** First letter of your name recognition. Simply hold up a letter and ask children to line-up/transition if their name starts with the letter	Letter cards (made or bought)	Assessment
Cognitive Development	------	**Extension Center:**		Photo Assessment
Cognitive Development		*What was successful and interesting to students last week? Carry this over to a center this week, so the students may extend this play/learning.* **Provocation:** Kwanzaa colors. Provide students with a black sheet of construction paper, glue/glue sticks, and geometric shapes cut-out of red, green, and yellow construction paper.	glue/glue sticks, black, red, green, yellow construction paper	Photo Assessment
Language Development Cognitive Development Home Connection Fine Motor Development Social/Emotional Dev.		**Morning Meeting:** 1. Good morning song (Teacher's choice) 2. Monday: Morning Message **Letter/Word Focus:** Ff, Me 3. Tues-Fri: **"My News"** **/Writing Prompt:** What makes you smile? _____makes me smile.	Music device, white-board, chart paper, sharpie, dry-erase marker	Photo Assessment

STANDARDS	TIME	OUTDOOR ACTIVITIES	MATERIALS	DOCUMENTATION
Social/Emotional Dev. Language Development Cognitive Development Sensory Development Gross Motor Development		**Outdoor time/Free Choice:** *Optional activities include: watering plants, pulling weeds, gardening, sensory, snow painting, snowman building, snow shoveling, raking leaves, etc.*		Photo Assessment

99

Extra Activities:

STANDARDS	TIME	LEARNING CENTER ACTIVITY CHOICES	MATERIALS	DOCUMENTATION
Language Development Cognitive Development Home Connection Fine Motor Development		**WRITING:** Name, Letter Focus, My News/Writing Prompt. Use relevant writing sheets to complete writing time or allow the students time to freely draw and the teacher to dictate the students' drawing. Teacher can use the dictation to encourage identification of letters and words along with independent writing.	Highlighter, pencils or crayons	Photo Assessment
Cognitive Development Sensory Development		**SENSORY:** Jingle Bell Bin. Place the jingle bells and the shredded paper into a bin along with different size containers with lids. Let the children explore by placing the bells into the different containers and shaking them to hear the different sounds	Jingle bells, decorative crinkle shred paper (red, yellow and green)	Photo Assessment
Language Development Cognitive Development Fine Motor Development Gross Motor Social/Emotional Dev.		**Learning Centers:** *Note any changes and/or additions made to learning centers*		Photo Assessment
Language Development Cognitive Development Sensory Development Fine Motor Development		**PROCESS ART:** African necklaces. Take a paper plate and cut out the middle, leaving the ridged edges. Cut through one side of the circle so that the student will be able to open the circle to place around his/her neck in necklace fashion. Provide	Paper plates, watercolors, paint brushes	Photo Assessment

100

STANDARDS	TIME	ACTIVITIES	MATERIALS	DOCUMENTATION
		students with paper plate necklace and bright watercolors. Allow the student to paint the necklace. **Question:** Why does your sock sometimes stick to your sweater when it comes out of the dryer? Why does your hair sometimes stand up when you put on a shirt?	Blown-up balloons, tinsel, and cut tissue paper.	Photo Assessment
Language Development Cognitive Development Sensory Development Fine Motor Development Social/Emotional Dev.		**View:** Use the internet or a book to view static electricity with balloons		
		STEM/STEAM PROJECT: Static Electricity. Provide the student with a blown-up balloon. Tell the students that every object is made up of energy and we are going to move the energy from one object to another. Have students first rub the balloon on their heads and then test it on their hair. Have the students test the balloon by touching it to a small piece of tinsel, small piece of tissue paper and other objects throughout the classroom. Why does it stick to some objects and not others?		

STANDARDS	TIME	CIRCLE TIME ACTIVITIES	MATERIALS	DOCUMENTATION
Cognitive Development Language Development Gross Motor Development Social/Emotional Dev.		**CIRCLE TIME:** 1. Calendar Activities (Days, Months, Counting, Patterns, Season, Year) -Do jumping jacks while counting the days of the month	Calendar, colored calendar numbers, music source	Photo Assessment
Cognitive Development Language Development Social/Emotional Dev.		**2.** Music & Movement: **Story Time:** Books about Kwanzaa, holidays around the world, electricity, Africa		Photo Assessment

13. Relevant Writing 1

*Write with a highlighter so child can trace if needed.

Name Recognition and Practice

_____

Letter Recognition and Practice

F_____

f_____

me_____

13. Relevant Writing 2

*Write the student's news on the line below using a highlighter.

_____

*Encourage student to draw a picture of their news below.

13. Week 13 Shopping List

ITEMS	YES, we have this item	NO, we need to buy	$ COST Of item	ITEMS	YES, we have this item	NO, we need to buy	$ COST Of item
PROVOCATION: glue/glue sticks black, red green, yellow construction paper **MORNING MEETING:** Music device White-board chart paper sharpie dry-erase marker **WRITING:** Highlighter chart paper Pencils				SENSORY: Jingle bells decorative crinkle shred paper (red, yellow and green) **PROCESS ART:** Paper plates watercolors paint brushes **STEAM:** Blown-up balloons tinsel tissue paper			

13. Parent Letter

Dear Family,

This week your child will learn about Kwanzaa a secular festival observed by many African Americans from December 26 to January 1 as a celebration of their cultural heritage and traditional values. They will also explore static electricity!

Provocation: Kwanzaa Colors	Sensory: Jingle Bell Bin	Letter/Word Focus: F, Me
Process Art: African Necklaces	STEM Project: Static Electricity	Writing: _____ makes me smile!

DATE: _____ WEEK #: _14_ TITLE: __Hanukkah__ TEACHER: _____

DAILY SCHEDULE & PLANS

STANDARDS	TIME	DAILY ACTIVITIES	MATERIALS	DOCUMENTATION
Cognitive Development Language Development	------	**Weekly Transition:** Have students who have laces on their shoes, buttons on their shirt, bows in their hair, etc. transition to the next activity or line-up.		Assessment
Cognitive Development	------	**Extension Center:**		Assessment Photo
Cognitive Development		*What was successful and interesting to students last week? Carry this over to a center this week, so the students may extend this play/learning.* **Provocation:** Hanukkah paper chain. Cut out blue and white strips of paper and provide glue sticks for children to begin making patterned paper chains using the colors of Hanukkah. These chains can be shaped into a Menorah or just used to decorate the classroom.	Glue sticks, blue & white construction paper	Assessment Photo
Cognitive Development Language Development Social/Emotional Dev. Fine Motor Development		**Morning Meeting:** 1. Good morning song (Teacher's choice) 2. Monday: Morning Message **Letter/Word Focus:** Bb, big 3. Tues-Fri: **"My News"/Writing Prompt:** What is something that is big? _____ is big.	Music device, white-board, chart paper, sharpie, dry-erase marker	Assessment Photo

STANDARDS	TIME	OUTDOOR ACTIVITIES	MATERIALS	DOCUMENTATION
Cognitive Development Language Development Gross Motor Development Sensory Development Social/Emotional Dev.		**Outdoor time/Free Choice:** *Optional activities include: watering plants, pulling weeds, gardening, sensory, snow painting, snowman building, snow shoveling, raking leaves, collecting rocks, etc.*		Assessment Photo

108

Extra Activities:

STANDARDS	TIME	LEARNING CENTER ACTIVITY CHOICES	MATERIALS	DOCUMENTATION
Cognitive Development Language Development Fine Motor Development		**WRITING:** Name, Letter Focus, My News/Writing Prompt. Use relevant writing sheets to complete writing time or allow the students time to freely draw and the teacher to dictate the students' drawing. Teacher can use the dictation to encourage identification of letters and words along with independent writing.	Highlighter, pencils or crayons	Assessment Photo
Cognitive Development Sensory Development		**SENSORY:** Cookie dough play! Place 5 cups of flour, 1 cup of cooking oil, vanilla extract and sprinkles to the sensory bin. Allow the children to mix until they create cookie-smelling dough.	Flour, cooking oil, vanilla extract, sprinkles	Assessment Photo
Cognitive Development Language Development Gross Motor Development Sensory Development Social/Emotional Dev. Fine Motor Development		Learning Centers: *Note any changes and/or additions made to learning centers*		Assessment Photo
Cognitive Development Language Development Sensory Development Fine Motor Development		**PROCESS ART:** Star of David. Provide children with 6 craft sticks to paint and decorate with glitter or sequins. After student is finished, glue the sticks into 2 triangles. Place one triangle on top of the other to create a star shape.	Craft sticks, paint, glitter, sequins, hot glue, yarn	Assessment Photo

109

| | | | Jingle bells, clear jars with lids, clear carbonated soda, water | Assessment Photo |

Cognitive Development
Language Development
Sensory Development
Social/Emotional Dev.
Fine Motor Development

Question: Show children a jar of water and a jar of a clear carbonated drink. Ask them how they are alike and different. You can write these on a chart for display. Ask the children to then predict what will happen when you place the jingle bells in the water and then in the soda.

View: Use the internet to view raisins "dancing" in soda.

STEM/STEAM PROJECT:
Dancing Jingle Bells! Place a few jingle bells in the water jar and the carbonated beverage jar. Observe the two jars and discuss. Give each child a small jar and let them pour in some soda and add a few jingle bells. Let them observe their own jingle bells jumping up and down. Place a lid on top for take-home.

STANDARDS	TIME	CIRCLE TIME ACTIVITIES	MATERIALS	DOCUMENTATION
Cognitive Development Language Development Gross Motor Development Social/Emotional Dev.		**CIRCLE TIME:** 1. Calendar Activities (Days, Months, Counting, Patterns, Season, Year) -Clap the days of the month 2. Music & Movement:	Calendar, colored calendar numbers, music source	Assessment Photo
Cognitive Development Language Development Social/Emotional Dev.		**Story Time:** Books about December, Christmas, Kwanzaa, Hanukkah, and family		Assessment Photo

STANDARDS	TIME	EXTRA ACTIVITIES	MATERIALS	DOCUMENTATION

14. Relevant Writing 1

Name Recognition and Practice

_____

Letter Recognition and Practice

B_____

b_____

big_____

14. Relevant Writing 2

*Write the student's news on the line below using a highlighter.

_____

*Encourage student to draw a picture of their news below.

14. Week 14 Shopping List

ITEMS	YES, we have this item	NO, we need to buy	$ COST Of item	ITEMS	YES, we have this item	NO, we need to buy	$ COST Of item
PROVOCATION: Glue sticks blue & white construction paper				SENSORY: Flour cooking oil vanilla extract sprinkles			
MORNING MEETING: Music device White-board chart paper sharpie dry-erase marker				PROCESS ART: Craft sticks Paint Glitter Sequins hot glue Yarn			
WRITING: Highlighter chart paper Pencils				STEAM: Jingle bells clear jars with lids clear carbonated soda water			

14. Parent Letter

Dear Family,

This week your child will learn about Hanukkah, the Jewish holiday that is celebrated for eight days, in honor of the miracle of the oil that lasted eight days in the Holy Temple. Students will also explore dancing jingle bells!

Don't forget your child's glass jar and lid, so they may take home their dancing jingle bells! Thank you!

Provocation: Blue & white patterned paper chains	Sensory: Cookie cloud dough	Letter/Word Focus: Bb, Big
Process Art: Star ornament	STEM Project: Dancing jingle bells	Writing: I want a big_____.

DATE: _____ WEEK #: _15_ TITLE: __Christmas__ TEACHER: _____

DAILY SCHEDULE & PLANS

STANDARDS	TIME	DAILY ACTIVITIES	MATERIALS	DOCUMENTATION
Cognitive Development Language Development	-------	**Weekly Transition:** # recognition. Hold up numbers 1-10 and ask the student what the number is when transitioning.	Homemade number cards or flashcards	Assessment
	-------	**Extension Center:**		Assessment Photo
Cognitive Development				
		What was successful and interesting to students last week? Carry this over to a center this week, so the students may extend this play/learning.		
Cognitive Development		**Provocation:** Seasonal sticky table art. Place a long piece of contact paper sticky-side up on the table. Secure the ends and edges with tape, so that it cannot easily be pulled up. Use a tray with dividers or small bowls to fill with exciting art pieces. Example: Green felt triangles, 3-4" chenille sticks, pom poms, and any other extra materials you have lying around. Do not give too many choices as it may overwhelm your little learners. Allow them to stick, create and explore with the materials on the contact paper.	Contact paper, green felt, pom poms, chenille sticks, tape	Assessment Photo
Cognitive Development Language Development Home Connection Fine Motor Development		**Morning Meeting:** 1. Good morning song (Teacher's choice) 2. Monday: Morning Message **Letter/Word Focus:** Nn, Run 3. Tues-Fri: **"My News"/Writing Prompt:** Where can you run to? I can run to _____.	Music device, white-board, chart paper, sharpie, dry-erase marker	Assessment Photo

STANDARDS	TIME	OUTDOOR ACTIVITIES	MATERIALS	DOCUMENTATION
Cognitive Development Language Development Gross Motor Development Sensory Development		**Outdoor time/Free Choice:** *Optional activities include: watering plants, pulling weeds, gardening, sensory, snow painting, snowman building, snow shoveling, raking leaves, etc.*		Assessment Photo

116

Extra Activities:

STANDARDS	TIME	LEARNING CENTER ACTIVITY CHOICES	MATERIALS	DOCUMENTATION
Cognitive Development Language Development Home Connection Fine Motor Development		**WRITING:** Name, Letter Focus, My News. Use relevant writing sheets to complete writing time or allow the students time to freely draw and the teacher to dictate the students' drawings.	Highlighter, pencils, crayons	Assessment Photo
Cognitive Development Sensory Development		**SENSORY:** Candy cane salt tray. Students can use candy canes to draw in the salt	Candy canes, salt, tray	Assessment Photo
Cognitive Development Language Development Gross Motor Development Sensory Development Fine Motor Development		**Learning Centers:** *Note any changes and/or additions made to learning centers*		Assessment Photo
Cognitive Development Language Development Fine Motor Development Sensory Development		**PROCESS ART:** Christmas Trees. Cut-out large triangles from card stock,, cut toilet paper rolls into 3 sections for dipping and printing, provide a few plates of different shades of green paint. Also, provide couple of bowls for tiny circles (can come from a hole-puncher) of different colors, and some short pieces of yarn to decorate the tree.	White cardstock, green paint, white paint, different color hole-punched paper, short pieces of yarn	Assessment Photo
Cognitive Development Language Development Fine Motor Development Sensory Development		**Question:** Show the students the ingredients to Ooblek. Asked them to predict what will happen when they mix the ingredients. Write down their predictions and revisit after you create the Ooblek.	Cornstarch, water, container for mixing, peppermints, spoons	Assessment Photo

View: Use the internet to view scientists mixing chemicals and producing chemical reactions.

STEM/STEAM PROJECT:
Candy cane Ooblek. You can begin the experiment in a large container, cook sheet or an individual bowl for each child. Mix together 1 cup cornstarch and ½ cup water. Let the children add the peppermints for cool color and smell. Give the students a spoon to begin mixing. Talk to students about how sometimes the mixture is a solid and sometimes a liquid!

STANDARDS	TIME	CIRCLE TIME ACTIVITIES	MATERIALS	DOCUMENTATION
Cognitive Development Language Development Gross Motor Development		**CIRCLE TIME:** **1.** Calendar Activities (Days, Months, Counting, Patterns, Season, Year) -March while counting the days of the month **2.** Music & Movement:	Calendar, colored calendar numbers, music source	Assessment Photo
Cognitive Development Language Development		**Story Time:** Books about December, Christmas, Kwanzaa, Hanukkah, and family		Assessment Photo

STANDARDS	TIME	EXTRA ACTIVITIES	MATERIALS	DOCUMENTATION

15. Relevant Writing 1

Name Recognition and Practice

_____

Letter Recognition and Practice

N_____

n _____

run_____

15. Relevant Writing 2

*Write the student's news on the line below using a highlighter.

---

*Encourage student to draw a picture of their news below.

15. Week 15 Shopping List

ITEMS	YES, we have this item	NO, we need to buy	$ COST Of item	ITEMS	YES, we have this item	NO, we need to buy	$ COST Of item
PROVOCATION: Contact paper green felt pom poms chenille sticks				SENSORY: Candy canes Salt tray			
tape **MORNING MEETING:** Music device White-board chart paper sharpie dry-erase marker				**PROCESS ART:** White cardstock green paint white paint different color hole-punched paper			
WRITING: Highlighter chart paper Pencils				short pieces of yarn **STEAM:** Cornstarch Water container for mixing			
				peppermints spoons			

15. Parent Letter

Dear Family,

This week your child is experiencing the sights, smells and sounds of Christmas! We will be making a special peppermint Ooblek for all! Did you know that Ooblek is both a solid and a liquid?

Provocation: Seasonal sticky table art	Sensory: Candy cane salt tray	Letter/Word Focus: Nn, Run
Process Art: Christmas Tree	STEM Project: Peppermint Ooblek	Writing: I run to_____.

DATE: _____ WEEK #: _16_ TITLE: __Ice__ TEACHER: _____

DAILY SCHEDULE & PLANS

STANDARDS	TIME	DAILY ACTIVITIES	MATERIALS	DOCUMENTATION
Cognitive Development Language Development	------	**Weekly Transition:** Phonics recognition. Make the letter sound and have the student guess the letter and/or vice versa.		Assessment
Cognitive Development	------	**Extension Center:**		Assessment Photo
Cognitive Development		*What was successful and interesting to students last week? Carry this over to a center this week, so the students may extend this play/learning.* **Provocation:** Make your own snowman. Place a black/blue piece of construction paper at each seat. Have bowls/baskets with the following: White circles, small black circles using a hole punch, orange triangles, colorful circles using a hole punch, black/brown squares and thin rectangles, glue sticks, and white chalk. Place a picture of snowman (printed or book) in the center of the table. Ask children to build their own snowman.	Black, brown, blue, white, orange, & multicolor construction paper, white chalk, glue sticks	Assessment Photo
Cognitive Development Language Development Social/Emotional Dev. Fine Motor Development		**Morning Meeting:** 1. Good morning song (Teacher's choice) 2. Monday: Morning Message **Letter/Word Focus:** Hh, can 3. Tues-Fri: **"My News"/Writing Prompt:** What can you do? I can _____.	Music device, white-board, chart paper, sharpie, dry-erase marker	Assessment Photo

STANDARDS	TIME	OUTDOOR ACTIVITIES	MATERIALS	DOCUMENTATION
Cognitive Development Language Development Gross Motor Development Sensory Development		**Outdoor time/Free Choice:** *Optional activities include: watering plants, pulling weeds, gardening, sensory, snow*		Assessment Photo

123

Social/Emotional Dev.

painting, snowman building,
snow shoveling, raking leaves,
etc.

Extra Activities:

STANDARDS	TIME	LEARNING CENTER ACTIVITY CHOICES	MATERIALS	DOCUMENTATION
Cognitive Development Language Development Fine Motor Development		**WRITING:** Name, Letter Focus, My News/Writing Prompt. Use relevant writing sheets to complete writing time or allow the students time to freely draw and the teacher to dictate the students' drawing. Teacher can use the dictation to encourage identification of letters and words along with independent writing.	Highlighter, pencils or crayons	Assessment Photo
Cognitive Development Sensory Development		**SENSORY:** Free the frozen animals/Letters. Freeze small plastic animals or letters in ice cube trays overnight. Place a small amount of cold water in the sensory bin. Then drop the ice cubes in the water. Provide students with child-safe tools such as wooden hammers to break the ice and free the animals. Students can wear safety goggles.	Ice trays, water, small plastic animals/letters, safety goggles	Assessment Photo
Cognitive Development Language Development Gross Motor Development Sensory Development Social/Emotional Dev. Fine Motor Development		**Learning Centers:** *Note any changes and/or additions made to learning centers*		Assessment Photo

Cognitive Development Language Development Sensory Development Fine Motor Development	**PROCESS ART:** Winter bubble wrap tree. Place a picture of a winter tree without its leaves in the center of the table. Talk about the shape and color of the trees in the winter. Give students a blue piece of construction paper/cardstock. Give them a black sharpie and ask them to carefully draw a winter tree. When they finish take the Sharpie and provide them with a small piece of bubble wrap, white paint, and paintbrush. Demonstrate painting the bubble wrap and printing it onto the tree as snow. Let them create their own snow prints.	White paint, paint brushes, bubble wrap, blue construction paper/cardstock, black Sharpies	Assessment Photo
Cognitive Development Language Development Sensory Development Social/Emotional Dev. Fine Motor Development	**Question:** What is ice made of?	Water, freezable containers, water beads	Assessment Photo
	View: Use internet or a book to show people skating on an outdoor ice rink.		
	STEM/STEAM PROJECT: Water beads on ice. Place small containers or one large container (for a group project) with just enough water to cover the bottom in the freezer overnight. Hand the students their own frozen container or group container and a cup full of water beads. Let them experiment with moving the water beads on the ice, trying to stack the water beads, feel the ice and beads. Listen and record their comments about the ice and beads for documentation. This activity can also be taken outside.		

STANDARDS	TIME	CIRCLE TIME ACTIVITIES	MATERIALS	DOCUMENTATION
Cognitive Development Language Development Gross Motor Development Social/Emotional Dev.		**CIRCLE TIME:** **1.** Calendar Activities (Days, Months, Counting, Number Patterns, Season, Year) **2.** Music & Movement:	Calendar, colored calendar numbers, music source	Assessment Photo
Cognitive Development Language Development Social/Emotional Dev.		**Story Time:** Books winter, snowmen, snow, ice, polar animals, hibernation, etc.		Assessment Photo

STANDARDS	TIME	EXTRA ACTIVITIES	MATERIALS	DOCUMENTATION

16. Relevant Writing 1

*Write with a highlighter so child can trace if needed.

Name Recognition and Practice

_____

Letter Recognition and Practice

H_____

h_____

can_____

16. Relevant Writing 2

*Write the student's news on the line below using a highlighter.

_____

*Encourage student to draw a picture of their news below.

16. Week 16 Shopping List

ITEMS	YES, we have this item	NO, we need to buy	$ COST Of item	ITEMS	YES, we have this item	NO, we need to buy	$ COST Of item
PROVOCATION: Black, brown, blue, white, orange, & multicolor construction paper				SENSORY: Ice trays Water			
white chalk glue sticks				small plastic animals/letters			
				safety goggles			
MORNING MEETING: Music device White-board chart paper sharpie dry-erase marker				PROCESS ART: White paint paint brushes bubble wrap blue construction paper/cardstock			
WRITING: Highlighter chart paper Pencils				black Sharpies STEAM: Water Shallow freezable containers			
				water beads			

16. Parent Letter

Dear Family,

Let's talk about WINTER! The thought of ice, snow and snowmen always intrigues young children. This week we will capture their curiosity by providing them with both a creative and scientific winter environment to explore!

Provocation: Make your own snowman	Sensory: Free the frozen animals	Letter/Word Focus: Hh, Can
Process Art: Winter bubble wrap trees	STEM Project: Water beads on ice	Writing: I can _____.

DATE: _____ WEEK #:_17_ TITLE: ___Let it snow___ TEACHER: _____

Daily Schedule

STANDARDS	TIME	DAILY ACTIVITIES	MATERIALS	DOCUMENTATION
Cognitive Development Language Development Fine Motor Development	------	**Weekly Transition:** Syllables. Clap each child's name and ask them how many claps are in their name. Slowly change the word "clap" to "syllables."		Assessment
Cognitive Development Sensory Development	------	**Extension Center:**		Assessment Photo
Cognitive Development Language Development Gross Motor Development Sensory Development Social/Emotional Dev. Fine Motor Development		*What was successful and interesting to students last week? Carry this over to a center this week, so the students may extend this play/learning.* **Provocation:** Draw your own snowflake. Draw one picture of an "X". Then draw a 2nd picture of an "X" with a line through the center from left to right resembling a snowflake shape. Laminate these and place on the table to help students understand how to draw a snowflake. Provide students with a glue bottle to trace their snowflake. Provide small bowl of sugar for the student to sprinkle the sugar on the glue to create a sparkly snowflake. Children may also create their own snow creations with the glue and sugar.	Glue bottles, sugar, construction paper, dark crayon or marker	Assessment Photo
Cognitive Development Language Development Social/Emotional Dev. Fine Motor Development		**Morning Meeting:** 1. Good morning song (Teacher's choice) 2. Monday: Morning Message **Letter/Word Focus:** Y, y; the 3. Tues-Fri: **"My News"** **Writing Prompt:** Tell me about snow. The snow is _____.	Music device, white-board, chart paper, sharpie, dry-erase marker	Assessment Photo

STANDARDS	TIME	OUTDOOR ACTIVITIES	MATERIALS	DOCUMENTATION
Cognitive Development Language Development Gross Motor Development Sensory Development		Outdoor time/Free Choice:		Assessment Photo

131

Social/Emotional Dev.

Optional activities include: watering plants, pulling weeds, gardening, sensory, snow painting, snowman building, snow shoveling, raking leaves, etc.

Extra Activities:

STANDARDS	TIME	LEARNING CENTER ACTIVITY CHOICES	MATERIALS	DOCUMENTATION
Cognitive Development Language Development Fine Motor Development		**WRITING:** Name, Letter Focus, My News/Writing Prompt. Use relevant writing sheets to complete writing time or allow the students time to freely draw and the teacher to dictate the students' drawing. Teacher can use the dictation to encourage identification of letters and words along with independent writing.	Highlighter, pencils or crayons	Assessment Photo
Cognitive Development Sensory Development		**SENSORY:** Fill the sensory bin with Insta Snow (make sure the label says it's safe for the children you are teaching) or you can use a bag of sugar and sugar cubes. Add small trucks, dump trucks and even small shovels and buckets for exploration.	Insta Snow/sugar, sugar cube, small trucks, small shovels, small buckets	Assessment Photo
Cognitive Development Language Development Gross Motor Development Sensory Development Social/Emotional Dev. Fine Motor Development		**Learning Centers:** *Note any changes and/or additions made to learning centers*		Assessment Photo

Cognitive Development
Language Development
Sensory Development
Fine Motor Development

PROCESS ART: Snowy woods. This project will take 2 weeks. Place a picture of a snowy woods with bare trees or you may draw your own on the table. Talk about how the trees and the snow look. Provide the students with a piece of cardboard/cardstock. Demonstrate to the students how to paint stripes on their paper to resemble bare trees in a woods. Provide them with paint brushes and black paint. Let them create their own woods of bare trees (Don't worry about their spacing or direction. Let them paint freely.) Next under supervision provide them a toothpick to scrape up and down their trees. This will create a bark look. This will need to dry for the 2nd half of the project next week.

Cardboard/cardstock. Black paint, toothpicks, paintbrushes

Assessment
Photo

Cognitive Development
Language Development
Sensory Development
Social/Emotional Dev.
Fine Motor Development

Question: What is snow made of?

Baking soda, shaving cream, nature pieces, bowls

Assessment
Photo

View: Use internet or a book to view snow falling from the sky

STEM/STEAM PROJECT: Fake snow. Provide one large container for the class and/or a small take-home bowl or container for each child. Let the students mix baking soda and shaving cream to create snow. Have them add just a little shaving cream at a time and knead until they get the consistency of snow. Next ask them to build a snowman or snow fort to take home. Provide some small twigs and nature pieces for decorating their snowman.

STANDARDS	TIME	CIRCLE TIME ACTIVITIES	MATERIALS	DOCUMENTATION
		CIRCLE TIME:	Calendar, colored calendar numbers, music source	Assessment
		1. Calendar Activities (Days, Months, Counting, Patterns, Season, Year)		Photo
Cognitive Development Language Development Gross Motor Development Social/Emotional Dev.				
		-Have students tap their head while counting the days of the month		
		2. Music & Movement:		
Cognitive Development Language Development Social/Emotional Dev.		**Story Time:** Books winter, snowmen, snow, ice, polar animals, hibernation, etc.		Assessment Photo

STANDARDS	TIME	EXTRA ACTIVITIES	MATERIALS	DOCUMENTATION

17. Relevant Writing 1

Name Recognition and Practice

_____

Letter Recognition and Practice

Y_____

y_____

the_____

17. Relevant Writing 2

*Write the student's news on the line below using a highlighter.

*Encourage student to draw a picture of their news below.

17. Week 17 Shopping List

ITEMS	YES, we have this item	NO, we need to buy	$ COST Of item	ITEMS	YES, we have this item	NO, we need to buy	$ COST Of item
PROVOCATION: Glue bottles Sugar construction paper dark crayon or marker MORNING MEETING: Music device White-board chart paper sharpie dry-erase marker WRITING: Highlighter chart paper Pencils				SENSORY: Insta Snow/sugar sugar cubes small trucks small shovels small buckets PROCESS ART: Cardboard/ Cardstock Black paint toothpicks paintbrushes STEAM: Baking soda shaving cream nature pieces bowls			

17. Parent Letter

Dear Family,

Let it SNOW! Most every child loves the snow. It seems so magical! This week we are providing our students with a variety of snow experiences from creating their own fake snow to exploring snowy art.

Provocation: Draw your own snowflake	Sensory: Snow shoveling	Letter/Word Focus: Yy, the
Process Art: Snowy woods week 1	STEM Project: Fake snow	Writing: The snow is _____.

Weekly Storyboard and Pictures

STANDARDS	TIME	DAILY ACTIVITIES	MATERIALS	DOCUMENTATION
Cognitive Development Language Development Fine Motor Development	------	**Weekly Transition:** Name recognition. Ask children to line up by showing a name on a name plate/card	Name Cards or Names printed on an index card	Assessment
Cognitive Development Sensory Development	------	**Extension Center:**		Assessment Photo
Cognitive Development Language Development Gross Motor Development Sensory Development Social/Emotional Dev. Fine Motor Development		*What was successful and interesting to students last week? Carry this over to a center this week, so the students may extend this play/learning.* **Provocation:** Ice painting. Use Tupperware or a freezable container to freeze water blocks overnight. Place the block of ice on a tray along with several colors of paints and a paintbrush. Let the children paint the block of ice.	Freezable containers, water, paint, paintbrushes, tray	Assessment Photo
Cognitive Development Language Development Social/Emotional Dev. Fine Motor Development		**Morning Meeting:** 1. Good morning song (Teacher's choice) 2. Monday: Morning Message Letter/Word Focus: Ss, is 3. Tues-Fri: "My News"/Writing Prompt: Tell me about winter. Winter is _____.	Music device, white-board, chart paper, sharpie, dry-erase marker	Assessment Photo

STANDARDS	TIME	OUTDOOR ACTIVITIES	MATERIALS	DOCUMENTATION
Cognitive Development Language Development Gross Motor Development Sensory Development Social/Emotional Dev.		**Outdoor time/Free Choice:** *Optional activities include: watering plants, pulling weeds, gardening, sensory, snow painting, snowman building, snow shoveling, raking leaves, etc.* **Extra Activities:**		Assessment Photo

STANDARDS	TIME	LEARNING CENTER ACTIVITY CHOICES	MATERIALS	DOCUMENTATION
Cognitive Development Language Development Fine Motor Development		**WRITING:** Name, Letter Focus, My News/Writing Prompt. Use relevant writing sheets to complete writing time or allow the students time to freely draw and the teacher to dictate the students' drawing. Teacher can use the dictation to encourage identification of letters and words along with independent writing.	Highlighter, pencils or crayons	Assessment Photo
Cognitive Development Sensory Development		**SENSORY:** Fill the sensory bin with blocks of ice, plastic polar animals, and cup of salt. Let the children explore the effect of the salt on the ice along with using their imagination to play with the polar animals on the ice.	Blocks of ice, plastic polar animals, salt in cups, and funnels	Assessment Photo
Cognitive Development Language Development Gross Motor Development Sensory Development Social/Emotional Dev. Fine Motor Development		**Learning Centers:** *Note any changes and/or additions made to learning centers*		Assessment Photo
Cognitive Development Language Development Sensory Development Fine Motor Development		**PROCESS ART:** Snowy woods. This is week 2 of this project. Take the dried trees the students painted last week and use painters' tape to tape it to the inside, bottom of a shoebox or other small box. Provide a small bowl of white paint with a little water mixed in. Let the student dip the brush in the paint and then tap the brush on the side of the shoebox so that the paint splatters onto the trees until the student is satisfied with his/her snowy trees.	White paint, paintbrushes, shoebox, painters' tape	Assessment Photo

140

STANDARDS		
Cognitive Development Language Development Sensory Development Social/Emotional Dev. Fine Motor Development	Remove the painting from the box to dry. **Question:** Show the students the ingredients. Ask them what they think you should do with the ingredients. Then ask them to name each ingredient. Explain that scientist mix ingredients to create something new. What do you think we can create with these ingredients? **View:** Scientist mixing chemicals and the results **STEM/STEAM PROJECT:** Fun putty. Mix 1 cup of cornstarch, food coloring, and ½ cup of dish soap in a bowl with a spoon until it becomes too hard to mix. Then let the children mix with their hands until it becomes fun putty. You may have to add more dish soap depending upon the consistency. Add slowly. You can send home the student's flubber in a ziplock bag.	Corn starch, food coloring, clear dish soap, medium-sized ziplock bags Assessment Photo

STANDARDS	TIME	CIRCLE TIME ACTIVITIES	MATERIALS	DOCUMENTATION
Cognitive Development Language Development Gross Motor Development Social/Emotional Dev.		**CIRCLE TIME:** 1. Calendar Activities (Days, Months, Counting, Patterns, Season, Year) -Hop on one foot while counting the days in the month	Calendar, colored calendar numbers, music source	Assessment Photo
Cognitive Development Language Development Social/Emotional Dev.		2. Music & Movement: **Story Time:** Books winter, snowmen, snow, ice, polar animals, hibernation, scientists, etc.		Assessment Photo

18. Relevant Writing 1

*Write with a highlighter so child can trace if needed.

Name Recognition and Practice

_____

Letter Recognition and Practice

S_____

s_____

Is_____

18. Relevant Writing 2

*Write the student's news on the line below using a highlighter.

*Encourage student to draw a picture of their news below.

18. Week 18 Shopping List

ITEMS	YES, we have this item	NO, we need to buy	$ COST Of item	ITEMS	YES, we have this item	NO, we need to buy	$ COST Of item
PROVOCATION: Freezable containers Water Paint Paintbrushes tray				SENSORY: Blocks of ice plastic polar animals salt in cups funnels			
MORNING MEETING: Music device White-board chart paper sharpie dry-erase marker				**PROCESS ART:** White paint paintbrushes shoebox painters' tape			
WRITING: Highlighter chart paper Pencils				**STEAM:** Corn starch food coloring clear dish soap medium-sized sealable plastic bags			

18. Parent Letter

Dear Family,

As the season continues, so does our study of ice, winter, and winter polar animals. Oh, beware of the FLUBBER/Silly Putty that your child will be making during STEM class! This can provide hours of fun for your child!

Provocation: Ice painting	Sensory: Polar animals on ice	Letter/Word Focus: Ss, is
Process Art: Snowy woods week 2	STEM Project: Fun putty	Writing: Winter is _____.

Weekly Storyboard and Pictures

STANDARDS	TIME	DAILY ACTIVITIES	MATERIALS	DOCUMENTATION
Cognitive Development Language Development Fine Motor Development	------	**Weekly Transition:** Rhyming. Pick a word such as "cat" and have each child give you a word that rhymes with "cat". Silly words count, too!		Assessment
Cognitive Development Sensory Development	------	**Extension Center:**		Assessment Photo
Cognitive Development Language Development Gross Motor Development Sensory Development Social/Emotional Dev. Fine Motor Development		*What was successful and interesting to students last week? Carry this over to a center this week, so the students may extend this play/learning.* **Provocation:** Winter, nature playdough. Provide students with homemade playdough (They could help make dough on the first day or during their sensory time) and add essential oils or spice such as cinnamon, clove or allspice. Add a few bowls of small sticks, pinecones, mountain animals (bears, coyotes, dogs, etc.), and small pieces of pines for trees. Then let them create their own scene! *Be sure to check for student allergies before adding any elements	Mountain animals, playdough, pinecones, pine bows	Assessment Photo
Cognitive Development Language Development Social/Emotional Dev. Fine Motor Development		**Morning Meeting:** 1. Good morning song (Teacher's choice) 2. Monday: Morning Message **Letter/Word Focus:** Pp, said 3. Tues-Fri: **"My News"** **/Writing Prompt:** What did Mom/Dad say to you this morning…. Mom/Dad said _____.	Music device, white-board, chart paper, sharpie, dry-erase marker	Assessment Photo

147

STANDARDS	TIME	OUTDOOR ACTIVITIES	MATERIALS	DOCUMENTATION
Cognitive Development Language Development Gross Motor Development Sensory Development Social/Emotional Dev.		**Outdoor time/Free Choice:** *Optional activities include: watering plants, pulling weeds, gardening, sensory, snow painting, snowman building, snow shoveling, raking leaves, etc.* **Extra Activities:**		Assessment Photo

STANDARDS	TIME	LEARNING CENTER ACTIVITY CHOICES	MATERIALS	DOCUMENTATION
Cognitive Development Language Development Fine Motor Development		**WRITING:** Name, Letter Focus, My News/Writing Prompt. Use relevant writing sheets to complete writing time or allow the students time to freely draw and the teacher to dictate the students' drawing. Teacher can use the dictation to encourage identification of letters and words along with independent writing.	Highlighter, pencils or crayons	Assessment Photo
Cognitive Development Sensory Development		**SENSORY:** Make playdough. Mix 1 cup flour, ¼ cup salt and 1 Tbsp. cream of tartar. If you are making one color batch add food coloring and essential oil/spice to the water then mix. If you plan to make 2 or more colors just mix in the water and add color and scent after dividing in half.	Flour, salt, cream of tartar, food coloring, and spice/essential oil.	Assessment Photo
Cognitive Development Language Development Gross Motor Development Sensory Development Social/Emotional Dev. Fine Motor Development		**Learning Centers:** *Note any changes and/or additions made to learning centers*		Assessment Photo
Cognitive Development Language Development Sensory Development Fine Motor Development		**PROCESS ART:** Melting Snowman. Thin some white tempera paint so it will go on thick, but can be blown using a straw. Provide the children with construction paper and a spoon. Use a book or picture of a snowman to show the students what a snowman looks like. Then ask them to use the spoon to spoon out the white paint and create their snowman. Provide	Straws, white paint, plastic spoons, construction paper, buttons/googly eyes, or paper cut-outs	Assessment Photo

148

Cognitive Development
Language Development
Sensory Development
Social/Emotional Dev.
Fine Motor Development

buttons, pom poms, googly eyes, and/or pieces of cut construction paper for the student to decorate the snowman (eyes, hat, nose, etc.). Then give the student a straw and let them blow the white paint until their snowman has melted!! Dictate the child's story about the snowman.

Question: Introduce the ingredients to the students and then ask them to predict what will happen when you combine the ingredients. Write the predictions on a board or chart paper.

View: Show the students crystals using the internet and talk to them about the aesthetics. Then let them know they will be growing their own crystals in their punch cup.

STEM/STEAM PROJECT: Grow Crystals. Provide each student with a clear plastic cup (punch cups are perfect) and a chenille stick/pipe-cleaner. Ask the student to create a design with the pipe-cleaner and then place it in the punch cup. Teacher should use one deep bowl to mix ½ cup Epsom Salt and ½ cup of hot tap water (just as hot as the tap water will get). Supervising allow each student to stir the mixture and observe the salt dissolving. Next give each student a scoop of the Epsom salt water and let them pour it into their own punch cup. Allow them to pick a food coloring they would like and mix in. Place in the refrigerator for 3 hours then take out to observe or observe the next day. You should be able to remove the pipe-cleaner with the crystals from the cup for a closer observation. Review the predictions written on the chart paper.

Epsom salt, warm water, chenille sticks, food coloring, bowl, clear punch cups, spoon for stirring

Assessment
Photo

STANDARDS	TIME	CIRCLE TIME ACTIVITIES	MATERIALS	DOCUMENTATION
Cognitive Development Language Development Gross Motor Development Social/Emotional Dev.		**CIRCLE TIME:** **1.** Calendar Activities (Days, Months, Counting, Patterns, Season, Year) --Balance on one foot while counting the months in the year	Calendar, colored calendar numbers, music source	Assessment Photo
Cognitive Development Language Development Social/Emotional Dev.		**2.** Music & Movement: **Story Time:** Books winter, snowmen, snow, ice, polar animals, hibernation, mountains, etc.		Assessment Photo

STANDARDS	TIME	EXTRA ACTIVITIES	MATERIALS	DOCUMENTATION

150

19. Relevant Writing 1

*Write with a highlighter so child can trace if needed.

Name Recognition and Practice

_____

Letter Recognition and Practice

P_____

p_____

said_____

19. Relevant Writing 2

*Write the student's news on the line below using a highlighter.

---

*Encourage student to draw a picture of their news below.

19. Week 19 Shopping List

ITEMS	YES, we have this item	NO, we need to buy	$ COST Of item	ITEMS	YES, we have this item	NO, we need to buy	$ COST Of item
PROVOCATION: Mountain animals playdough Pinecones pine bows				**SENSORY:** Flour Salt, cream of tartar food coloring spice/essential oil.			
MORNING MEETING: Music device White-board chart paper sharpie dry-erase marker				**PROCESS ART:** Straws white paint, plastic spoons construction paper			
WRITING: Highlighter chart paper Pencils				buttons/googly eyes or paper cut-outs **STEAM:** Epsom salt warm water chenille sticks food coloring bowl, clear punch cups spoon			

19. Parent Letter

Dear Family,

Let's talk about melting snowmen and growing crystals! Yes, your child is going to grow crystals in their STEAM class this week. Hopefully some will make it home.

Provocation: Winter, nature playdough scenes	Sensory: Homemade smelly playdough	Letter/Word Focus: Pp, said
Process Art: Melting snowmen	STEM Project: Growing crystals	Writing: Mom/Dad said _____.

Weekly Storyboard and Pictures

STANDARDS	TIME	DAILY ACTIVITIES	MATERIALS	DOCUMENTATION
Cognitive Development Language Development Fine Motor Development	------	**Weekly Transition:** # recognition. Use # cards or numbers written on stones to create a recognition game for transitions. Simply hold up the number and ask the child to identify before transitioning.	Index cards Sharpie	Assessment
Cognitive Development Sensory Development	------	**Extension Center:**		Assessment Photo
Cognitive Development Language Development Gross Motor Development Sensory Development Social/Emotional Dev. Fine Motor Development		*What was successful and interesting to students last week? Carry this over to a center this week, so the students may extend this play/learning.* **Provocation:** Love letters. Provide paper, pens, pencils and envelopes and help students write letters to their friends and family.	Envelopes, paper, pens, pencils	Assessment Photo
Cognitive Development Language Development Social/Emotional Dev. Fine Motor Development		**Morning Meeting:** 1. Good morning song (Teacher's choice) 2. Monday: Morning Message **Letter/Word Focus:** Ww, love 3. Tues-Fri: **"My News"** **/Writing Prompt:** Who do you love? I love _____.	Music device, white-board, chart paper, sharpie, dry-erase marker	Assessment Photo

STANDARDS	TIME	OUTDOOR ACTIVITIES	MATERIALS	DOCUMENTATION
Cognitive Development Language Development Gross Motor Development Sensory Development Social/Emotional Dev.		**Outdoor time/Free Choice:** *Optional activities include: watering plants, pulling weeds, gardening, sensory, snow painting, snowman building, snow shoveling, raking leaves, etc.*		Assessment Photo

155

Extra Activities:

STANDARDS	TIME	LEARNING CENTER ACTIVITY CHOICES	MATERIALS	DOCUMENTATION
Cognitive Development Language Development Fine Motor Development		WRITING: Name, Letter Focus, My News/Writing Prompt. Use relevant writing sheets to complete writing time or allow the students time to freely draw and the teacher to dictate the students' drawing. Teacher can use the dictation to encourage identification of letters and words along with independent writing.	Highlighter, pencils or crayons	Assessment Photo
Cognitive Development Sensory Development		SENSORY: Hot chocolate! Pour instant hot cocoa mix into a sensory bin along with marshmallows or Valentine hearts. Encourage students to use spoons and cups for exploration. Add measuring spoons and funnels.	Valentine hearts, hot cocoa mix, spoons, and cups/plastic mugs, measuring spoons, funnels	Assessment Photo
Cognitive Development Language Development Gross Motor Development Sensory Development Social/Emotional Dev. Fine Motor Development		Learning Centers: *Note any changes and/or additions made to learning centers		Assessment Photo
Cognitive Development Language Development		PROCESS ART: Group Paint! Provide students with	Tempera paint, bowls, butcher paper, music	Assessment Photo

STANDARDS	TIME	CIRCLE TIME	MATERIALS	DOCUMENTATION

Sensory Development
Fine Motor Development

one large piece of butcher paper. Roll it out on a table or floor. Tape down the edges using masking tape. Provide bowls or plates of tempera paint. Use paints that mix well such as red, pink, white or yellow, blue, white. Always add white to the mix to keep the mural from turning gray and black. Provide smocks for the students, put on some soft soothing music such as a meditation music, turn the lights down, and let them finger paint until their heart's content.

Cognitive Development
Language Development
Sensory Development
Social/Emotional Dev.
Fine Motor Development

Question: Show the students a catapult that you made. Ask the students how far they think you can catapult a conversation heart. Mark the distance on the floor or rug with tape and the name of the student. Perform the experiment and see who was closest!

Plastic spoons, conversation hearts or rocks, blocks, sticks, measuring tape

Assessment
Photo

View: Use the internet to provide video of homemade catapults in action.

STEM/STEAM PROJECT: Catapult. Simply place a spoon on the table and set a Valentine conversation candy heart or something small onto the head of the spoon. Place a small block or thick stick under the neck of the spoon. Ask a student to slap the end of the spoon that is up in the air and observe the conversation heart fly through the air! Provide the student with a plastic spoon, blocks, sticks, and candy hearts and see what kind of catapults they can build. You may also provide a line where the catapults can be placed and use a measuring tape to measure the distance. Which catapult flies the farthest or highest?

STANDARDS	TIME	CIRCLE TIME	MATERIALS	DOCUMENTATION

ACTIVITIES			
Cognitive Development Language Development Gross Motor Development Social/Emotional Dev.	**CIRCLE TIME:** 1. Calendar Activities (Days, Months, Counting, Patterns, Season, Year) - do jumping jacks while counting the days of the month	Calendar, colored calendar numbers, music source	Assessment Photo
Cognitive Development Language Development Social/Emotional Dev.	2. Music & Movement: **Story Time:** Books about Valentine's, love, friendship, family, and sharing.		Assessment Photo

STANDARDS	TIME	EXTRA ACTIVITIES	MATERIALS	DOCUMENTATION

20. Relevant Writing 1

*Write with a highlighter so child can trace if needed.

Name Recognition and Practice

_____

Letter Recognition and Practice

W_____

w_____

love_____

20. Relevant Writing 2

*Write the student's news on the line below using a highlighter.

---

*Encourage student to draw a picture of their news below.

20. Week 20 Shopping List

ITEMS	YES, we have this item	NO, we need to buy	$ COST Of item	ITEMS	YES, we have this item	NO, we need to buy	$ COST Of item
PROVOCATION: Envelopes Paper Pens pencils				SENSORY: .Valentine hearts hot cocoa mix Spoons cups/plastic mugs measuring spoons funnels			
MORNING MEETING: Music device White-board chart paper sharpie dry-erase marker				PROCESS ART: Tempera paint bowls butcher paper music STEAM: Plastic spoons, conversation hearts blocks Sticks measuring tape			
WRITING: Highlighter chart paper Pencils							

20. Parent Letter

Dear Family,

Catapults! Catapults are physics that children many times discover on their own through play. This week we are going to intentionally let them launch items across the room!

Provocation: Love letters	**Sensory:** Let's make Hot Chocolate!	**Letter/Word Focus:** Ww, Love
Process Art: Group Finger Paint	**STEM Project:** Catapults	**Writing:** I love_____.

DAILY SCHEDULE & PLANS

STANDARDS	TIME	DAILY ACTIVITIES	MATERIALS	DOCUMENTATION
Cognitive Development Language Development Fine Motor Development	------	**Weekly Transition:** 1st Letter of their name. Use letter cards or stones with letters on them (can be done with a Sharpie) and hold up the letter. Ask who's name starts with the letter you are holding.	Letter cards or letter stones	Assessment
Cognitive Development Sensory Development	------	**Extension Center:**		Assessment Photo
Cognitive Development Language Development Gross Motor Development Sensory Development Social/Emotional Dev. Fine Motor Development		*What was successful and interesting to students last week? Carry this over to a center this week, so the students may extend this play/learning.* **Provocation:** Friendship bracelets. Provide the students with a bowl of pony beads and chenille sticks. Allow the student to choose the color of their bracelet (chenille stick) and begin adding beads. You may demonstrate patterns or provide examples of patterns and ask the students to create a pattern for their friendship bracelet. Students can trade bracelets or make as a gift for someone special.	Pony beads, pipe-cleaners (chenille sticks)	Assessment Photo
Cognitive Development Language Development Social/Emotional Dev. Fine Motor Development		**Morning Meeting:** 1. Good morning song (Teacher's choice) 2. Monday: Morning Message 　**Letter/Word Focus:** Jj, We 3. Tues-Fri: **"My News"** /**Writing Prompt:** What do you like to do with your family? We like to _____.	Music device, white-board, chart paper, sharpie, dry-erase marker	Assessment Photo

163

STANDARDS	TIME	OUTDOOR ACTIVITIES	MATERIALS	DOCUMENTATION
Cognitive Development Language Development Gross Motor Development Sensory Development Social/Emotional Dev.		Outdoor time/Free Choice: *Optional activities include: watering plants, pulling weeds, gardening, sensory, snow painting, snowman building, snow shoveling, raking leaves, etc.* **Extra Activities:**		Assessment Photo

STANDARDS	TIME	LEARNING CENTER ACTIVITY CHOICES	MATERIALS	DOCUMENTATION
Cognitive Development Language Development Fine Motor Development		**WRITING:** Name, Letter Focus, My News/Writing Prompt. Use relevant writing sheets to complete writing time or allow the students time to freely draw and the teacher to dictate the students' drawing. Teacher can use the dictation to encourage identification of letters and words along with independent writing.	Highlighter, pencils or crayons	Assessment Photo
Cognitive Development Sensory Development		**SENSORY:** Mail it! Add packing peanuts to the sensory bin. Provide small boxes and packaging materials for pretend play. Students can pretend to package goods just like the post office. Tape is an option if closely supervised.	Packing peanuts, small boxes, packaging materials, tape	Assessment Photo
Cognitive Development Language Development Gross Motor Development Sensory Development Social/Emotional Dev. Fine Motor Development		**Learning Centers:** *Note any changes and/or additions made to learning centers*		Assessment Photo

Cognitive Development	PROCESS ART: Toe-tal	Masking tape, construction	Assessment
Language Development	Love! Cut large hearts out of	paper, washable paint, wide-	Photo
Sensory Development	construction paper or	mouth bowls	
Fine Motor Development	cardstock. Use masking tape		

Cognitive Development
Language Development
Sensory Development
Fine Motor Development

PROCESS ART: Toe-tal Love! Cut large hearts out of construction paper or cardstock. Use masking tape to tape the heart to the floor (a floor area that can be easily cleaned). Provide washable paint (pink, white, red) in wide-mouthed bowls. Have students take off their shoes and socks and let them paint their hearts using their toes!

Masking tape, construction paper, washable paint, wide-mouth bowls

Assessment
Photo

Cognitive Development
Language Development
Sensory Development
Social/Emotional Dev.
Fine Motor Development

Question: Before class, create a piece of marbled paper and let it dry. During class hold up a blank piece of paper in one hand and the marbled paper in the other hand. Have the students try and guess how you created the colors on the marbled paper.

Almond milk, watercolor paper or heavy construction paper (white.manilla), casserole dish/shallow pan, dish soap, food coloring or watercolors

Assessment
Photo

View: Use the internet to view a professional artist creating marbled paper

STEM/STEAM PROJECT: Marbled Milk Hearts/Cards. Cut watercolor paper or heavy construction paper (white or manilla) into hearts or rectangles that can folded to make a small card for someone special. Use a casserole dish or shallow pan and place almond milk in the bottom. You just need enough to cover the bottom of the dish. While supervising, allow the student to add drops of food coloring or watercolors to the milk. Add a few drops of dish soap to the mix and observe the interaction between the soap and the colors. Next, let the student use a q-tip or toothpick to swirl the colors around. Before the colors get too mixed have the student take the heart or rectangle paper and gently lay on top of the mixture. Press the paper just enough so that the front side of the paper is covered in the milk mixture. Set the paper aside to dry. Continue this process. When paper dries. Allow the student to write a note to someone special or dictate the note for the student.

STANDARDS	TIME	CIRCLE TIME ACTIVITIES	MATERIALS	DOCUMENTATION
Cognitive Development Language Development Gross Motor Development Social/Emotional Dev.		**CIRCLE TIME:** 1. Calendar Activities (Days, Months, Counting, Patterns, Season, Year) -Have the children shake their hips from side to side as they count the days of the month	Calendar, colored calendar numbers, music source	Assessment Photo
Cognitive Development Language Development Social/Emotional Dev.		2. Music & Movement: **Story Time:** Books about friends, friendship, family, love, Valentine's		Assessment Photo

STANDARDS	TIME	EXTRA ACTIVITIES	MATERIALS	DOCUMENTATION

166

21. Relevant Writing 1

*Write with a highlighter so child can trace if needed.

Name Recognition and Practice

_____

Letter Recognition and Practice

J_____

j_____

we_____

21. Relevant Writing 2

*Write the student's news on the line below using a highlighter.

_____

*Encourage student to draw a picture of their news below.

21. Week 21 Shopping List

ITEMS	YES, we have this item	NO, we need to buy	$ COST Of item	ITEMS	YES, we have this item	NO, we need to buy	$ COST Of item
PROVOCATION: Pony beads pipe-cleaners (chenille sticks) **MORNING MEETING:** Music device White-board chart paper sharpie dry-erase marker **WRITING:** Highlighter chart paper Pencils				**SENSORY:** .Packing peanuts small boxes packaging materials Tape **PROCESS ART:** Masking tape construction paper washable paint wide-mouth bowls **STEAM:** Almond milk watercolor paper or heavy construction paper (white or manilla) casserole dish/shallow pan dish soap food coloring Or watercolors			

21. Parent Letter

Dear Family,

Valentine's is the perfect time to talk to your child about LOVE! Love is family, friends, sharing, giving, and nice words! Let your child know how much you love them by making them homemade card. They will be so excited!

Provocation: Friendship Bracelets	Sensory: Mail it! Experience packaging items just like a postal worker!	Letter/Word Focus: I, We
Process Art: Toe-tal Love! Painting with our toes!	STEM Project: Marbled Milk	Writing: We like to _____.

DATE: _____ WEEK #:_22_ TITLE: __Dental Health__ TEACHER: _____

DAILY SCHEDULE & PLANS

STANDARDS	TIME	DAILY ACTIVITIES	MATERIALS	DOCUMENTATION
Cognitive Development Language Development Fine Motor Development	------	**Weekly Transition:** Phonics Recognition. Call on a student and make a letter sound. Ask the student to identify what letter makes that sound.		Assessment
Cognitive Development Sensory Development	------	**Extension Center:**		Assessment Photo
Cognitive Development Language Development Gross Motor Development Sensory Development Social/Emotional Dev. Fine Motor Development		*What was successful and interesting to students last week? Carry this over to a center this week, so the students may extend this play/learning.* **Provocation:** Draw what you see. Print a couple of landscapes, either place them in a paper protector or laminate them and set them on a table. Provide students with pencils and only the crayons that resemble the colors on the landscapes. Ask the children to look at the pictures, ask what they see, then ask them to draw what they see.	Paper, pencils, crayons, landscape pictures printed or in a book	Assessment Photo
Cognitive Development Language Development Social/Emotional Dev. Fine Motor Development		**Morning Meeting:** 1. Good morning song (Teacher's choice) 2. Monday: Morning Message **Letter/Word Focus:** Kk, come 3. Tues-Fri: **"My News"** /Writing Prompt: Will you come to _____.	Music device, white-board, chart paper, sharpie, dry-erase marker	Assessment Photo

STANDARDS	TIME	OUTDOOR ACTIVITIES	MATERIALS	DOCUMENTATION
Cognitive Development Language Development Gross Motor Development Sensory Development Social/Emotional Dev.		**Outdoor time/Free Choice:** *Optional activities include: watering plants, pulling weeds, gardening, sensory, snow painting, snowman building,*		Assessment Photo

171

snow shoveling, raking leaves,
etc.
Extra Activities:

STANDARDS	TIME	LEARNING CENTER ACTIVITY CHOICES	MATERIALS	DOCUMENTATION
Cognitive Development Language Development Fine Motor Development		**WRITING:** Name, Letter Focus, My News/Writing Prompt. Use relevant writing sheets to complete writing time or allow the students time to freely draw and the teacher to dictate the students' drawing. Teacher can use the dictation to encourage identification of letters and words along with independent writing.	Highlighter, pencils or crayons	Assessment Photo
Cognitive Development Sensory Development		**SENSORY:** Toothpaste Slime! Squirt toothpaste into bowl, squirt a small amount of glue (size of silver dollar) beside toothpaste. Ask student to use the spoon to add a little glue at a time to the toothpaste until it begins to look and feel like slime. You can always add more glue if necessary. Ask the student to pick up the slime and play with it until it is no longer sticky. Talk about touch and smell.	Spoons, glue, toothpaste, bowl	Assessment Photo
Cognitive Development Language Development Gross Motor Development Sensory Development Social/Emotional Dev. Fine Motor Development		**Learning Centers:** *Note any changes and/or additions made to learning centers*		Assessment Photo
Cognitive Development Language Development Sensory Development Fine Motor Development		**PROCESS ART:** Brush your teeth. Using a Sharpie, draw a large tooth the size of the entire sheet of construction	Construction paper, white paint, toothbrushes and plates/bowls	Assessment Photo

STANDARDS		
Cognitive Development Language Development Sensory Development Social/Emotional Dev. Fine Motor Development	paper. Provide students with white paint and toothbrushes to paint their tooth. Older students may practice their cutting skills by cutting out the tooth when the paint dries. **STEM/STEAM PROJECT:** Elephant Toothpaste! Show students the ingredients and bottle. Tell them you are going to mix it together. Ask each student what they predict will happen. Have them draw their prediction on a piece of paper and label it "Prediction." Then follow the experiment. Take an empty 16 oz water bottle and fill it with a ½ cup of hydrogen peroxide, add one Tablespoon of liquid dish soap and swirl it around. In a separate cup combine warm water and yeast and mix for 30 seconds (Have students help and count to 30). Now pour the yeast water into the bottle using a funnel and watch what happens. Ask the students what happened and have them draw it on the backside of the paper and label it "Conclusion."	Packet of yeast, 16 oz water bottle, Tablespoon, hydrogen peroxide, warm water Assessment Photo

STANDARDS	TIME	CIRCLE TIME ACTIVITIES	MATERIALS	DOCUMENTATION
Cognitive Development Language Development Gross Motor Development Social/Emotional Dev.		**CIRCLE TIME:** 1. Calendar Activities (Days, Months, Counting, Number Patterns, Season, Year)	Calendar, colored calendar numbers, music source	Assessment Photo
Cognitive Development Language Development Social/Emotional Dev.		**2.** Music & Movement: **Story Time:** Books about Dental health, brushing teeth, going to the dentist.		Assessment Photo

22. Relevant Writing 1

*Write with a highlighter so child can trace if needed.

Name Recognition and Practice

_____

Letter Recognition and Practice

K_____

k_____

come_____

22. Relevant Writing 2

*Write the student's news on the line below using a highlighter.

_____

*Encourage student to draw a picture of their news below.

22. Week 22 Shopping List

ITEMS	YES, we have this item	NO, we need to buy	$ COST Of item	ITEMS	YES, we have this item	NO, we need to buy	$ COST Of item
PROVOCATION: Paper Pencils Crayons				**SENSORY:** Spoons Glue Toothpaste bowl			
landscape pictures printed or in a book				**PROCESS ART:** Construction paper white paint toothbrushes plates/bowls			
MORNING MEETING: Music device White-board chart paper sharpie dry-erase marker				**STEAM:** Packet of yeast 16 oz water bottle Tablespoon hydrogen peroxide warm water			
WRITING: Highlighter chart paper Pencils							

22. Parent Letter

Dear Family,

February is Dental Health month! This is a great time to schedule a cleaning or check-up for your child. It is also a great time to introduce healthy habits such as brushing and flossing twice a day.

Provocation: Draw what you see!	Sensory: Toothpaste Slime	Letter/Word Focus: Kk, Come
Process Art: Painting with Toothbrushes	STEM Project: Elephant Toothpaste!	Writing: Will you come to _____.

DATE: _____ WEEK #:___23_____ TITLE: _____Grass Heads_____

TEACHER:_____

DAILY SCHEDULE & PLANS

STANDARDS	TIME	DAILY ACTIVITIES	MATERIALS	DOCUMENTATION
Cognitive Development Language Development Fine Motor Development	------	**Weekly Transition:** Syllables. Clap each child's name and ask them how many claps are in their name. Slowly change the word "clap" to "syllables."		Assessment
Cognitive Development Sensory Development	------	**Extension Center:**		Assessment Photo
Cognitive Development Language Development Gross Motor Development Sensory Development Social/Emotional Dev. Fine Motor Development		*What was successful and interesting to students last week? Carry this over to a center this week, so the students may extend this play/learning.* **Provocation:** Still Life. Provide students with a display of spring flowers such as daffodils or tulips in a vase as a centerpiece on a table. Provide paint (only the colors of the still life) and a paintbrush for each paint color along with a sheet of construction paper. Ask the students to observe the flowers and discuss what they see. Then welcome them to paint their own flower picture.	Flowers, vase, paint, paintbrushes, white or manilla construction paper	Assessment Photo
Cognitive Development Language Development Social/Emotional Dev. Fine Motor Development		**Morning Meeting:** 1. Good morning song (Teacher's choice) 2. Monday: Morning Message **Letter/Word Focus:** Qq, see 3. Tues-Fri: **"My News"/ Writing Prompt:** What can you see outside? I see _____.	Music device, white-board, chart paper, sharpie, dry-erase marker	Assessment Photo

STANDARDS	TIME	OUTDOOR ACTIVITIES	MATERIALS	DOCUMENTATION
Cognitive Development Language Development Gross Motor Development Sensory Development Social/Emotional Dev.		**Outdoor time/Free Choice:**		Assessment Photo

*Optional activities include:

179

watering plants, pulling weeds, gardening, sensory, snow painting, snowman building, snow shoveling, raking leaves, etc.

Extra Activities:

STANDARDS	TIME	LEARNING CENTER ACTIVITY CHOICES	MATERIALS	DOCUMENTATION
Cognitive Development **Language Development** **Fine Motor Development**		**WRITING:** Name, Letter Focus, My News/Writing Prompt. Use relevant writing sheets to complete writing time or allow the students time to freely draw and the teacher to dictate the students' drawing. Teacher can use the dictation to encourage identification of letters and words along with independent writing.	Highlighter, pencils or crayons	Assessment Photo
Cognitive Development **Sensory Development**		**SENSORY:** Clean Mud! Let children help mix together 1 cup flour, 1 cup salt, 1 cup water, along with a squirt or 2 of black/brown tempera paint. Ask children to mix with their hands and enjoy the mud play!	Flour, salt, water, black/brown tempera paint	Assessment Photo
Cognitive Development **Language Development** **Gross Motor Development** **Sensory Development** **Social/Emotional Dev.** **Fine Motor Development**		**Learning Centers:** *Note any changes and/or additions made to learning centers*		

Cognitive Development Language Development Sensory Development Fine Motor Development	PROCESS ART: Flower Prints! Provide students with a variety of materials to print flowers. These materials can be the bottom of a water or soda bottle, cups, or other recycled materials. Provide paint and construction paper to dip the materials in and print. Once the flowers are printed students can use green paint or marker to draw stems onto their flowers.	Construction paper, tempera paints, and printing items (soda bottles, water bottles, other recycled materials)	Assessment Photo
Cognitive Development Language Development Sensory Development Social/Emotional Dev. Fine Motor Development	Question: What does a plant need to grow? View: Use the internet to view a plant growth time lapse video STEM/STEAM PROJECT: Grass Heads! Take a short piece of tights or panty-hose and let student fill one end with grass seed and then fill with potting soil. Tie a knot to hold the seed and dirt inside. Let student use a sharpie to draw a face. Decorate a yogurt cup, plastic cup or Styrofoam cup to place the dirt-filled stocking in and then let the student spray with water daily. Observe and chart the growth of the grass daily/weekly. When the grass is tall enough you may let the students use scissors to cut the Grass Head's hair!	Grass seed, panty-hose, spray bottle for water, potting soil, cup, sharpies	Assessment Photo

STANDARDS	TIME	CIRCLE TIME ACTIVITIES	MATERIALS	DOCUMENTATION
Cognitive Development Language Development Gross Motor Development Social/Emotional Dev.		**CIRCLE TIME:** **1.** Calendar Activities (Days, Months, Counting, Patterns, Season, Year) -Have the students squat for each number as they count the days in the month	Calendar, colored calendar numbers, music source	Assessment Photo
Cognitive Development Language Development Social/Emotional Dev.		**2.** Music & Movement: **Story Time:** Books spring, flowers, plants, gardens, dirt, rain, etc.		Assessment Photo

STANDARDS	TIME	EXTRA ACTIVITIES	MATERIALS	DOCUMENTATION

23. Relevant Writing 1

Name Recognition and Practice

_____

Letter Recognition and Practice

Q _____

q _____

What can you see with your eyes?

I see _____.

Sight word recognition and practice.

See

_____

*Encourage student to draw a picture of what they see on the next page.

23. Week 23 Shopping List

ITEMS	YES, we have this item	NO, we need to buy	$ COST Of item	ITEMS	YES, we have this item	NO, we need to buy	$ COST Of item
PROVOCATION: Flowers Vase paint paintbrushes white or manilla construction paper				SENSORY: Flour Salt water black/brown tempera paint			
MORNING MEETING: Music device White-board chart paper sharpie dry-erase marker				PROCESS ART: Construction paper, tempera paints printing items (soda bottles, water bottles, recycled materials)			
WRITING: Highlighter chart paper Pencils				STEAM: Grass seed panty-hose spray bottle for water potting soil Cup sharpies			

23. Parent Letter

Dear Family,

Let's start planting and growing our gardens for SPRING! This week your child will learn the planting process by planting grass seeds and growing their own Grass Head! These are hilarious! It is a fun way to teach children about the process of growing plants. You can talk with your child about where his/her food comes from and what the farmers may be doing to prepare for the growing season.

Provocation: Still Life Flowers	Sensory: Mud Fun!	Letter/Word Focus: Qq, See
Process Art: Flower Printmaking	STEM Project: Grass Heads	Writing: I see _____.

DAILY SCHEDULE & PLANS

STANDARDS	TIME	DAILY ACTIVITIES	MATERIALS	DOCUMENTATION
Cognitive Development Language Development Fine Motor Development	------	**Weekly Transition:** Birth month. Ask the students, "If you were born in the month of _____ then you may………. (line up, wash your hands, etc.,)"	It will be helpful to keep a list of birthdays nearby.	Assessment
Cognitive Development Sensory Development	------	**Extension Center:**		Assessment Photo
		What was successful and interesting to students last week? Carry this over to a center this week, so the students may extend this play/learning.		
Cognitive Development Language Development Gross Motor Development Sensory Development Social/Emotional Dev. Fine Motor Development		**Provocation:** Wind Experience. Provide student with a variety of objects such as pom poms, cotton balls, pebble, and paper clip along with a cookie sheet or something to contain the blowing experiment. Provide the student with a straw and teach them how to blow through the straw. Allow them to place different sized objects on the cookie sheet and try to use the straw to blow them to the opposite end of the table or cookie sheet.	Cookie sheet, straws, small objects of different weights such as pom poms, pebble, cotton ball, paper clip, etc.	Assessment Photo
Cognitive Development Language Development Social/Emotional Dev. Fine Motor Development		**Morning Meeting:** 1. Good morning song (Teacher's choice) 2. Monday: Morning Message **Letter/Word Focus:** Xx, little 3. Tues-Fri: **"My News"** **/Writing Prompt:** Can you think of something that is little? _____is little.	Music device, white-board, chart paper, sharpie, dry-erase marker	Assessment Photo

STANDARDS	TIME	OUTDOOR ACTIVITIES	MATERIALS	DOCUMENTATION
Cognitive Development Language Development Gross Motor Development Sensory Development Social/Emotional Dev.		Outdoor time/Free Choice:		Assessment Photo

Optional activities include: watering plants, pulling weeds, gardening, sensory, snow painting, snowman building, snow shoveling, raking leaves, etc.

Extra Activities:

STANDARDS	TIME	LEARNING CENTER ACTIVITY CHOICES	MATERIALS	DOCUMENTATION
Cognitive Development Language Development Fine Motor Development		**WRITING:** Name, Letter Focus, My News/Writing Prompt. Use relevant writing sheets to complete writing time or allow the students time to freely draw and the teacher to dictate the students' drawing. Teacher can use the dictation to encourage identification of letters and words along with independent writing.	Highlighter, pencils or crayons	Assessment Photo
Cognitive Development Sensory Development		**SENSORY:** Let it Rain! Take a few plastic/foam cups and use a thumbtack to poke several holes in the bottom of the cup. Place water and a some cotton balls in the sensory bin. Allow the children to fill the cups with water and simulate rain. The cotton balls can simulate clouds. The student can pick up the cotton balls and squeeze the rain out of add the cotton balls to the cups to explore the water cycle process.	Water, plastic/foam cups, cotton balls	Assessment Photo
Cognitive Development Language Development Gross Motor Development Sensory Development Social/Emotional Dev. Fine Motor Development		Learning Centers: *Note any changes and/or additions made to learning centers*		Assessment Photo

Cognitive Development Language Development Sensory Development Fine Motor Development	**PROCESS ART:** Rainstorm. Provide students with tempera paint colors that would simulate rain such as a drop of blue, white and black. Provide student with several pieces (about 6" each) of cut yarn. Turn on a video or music with the sounds of rain and a rainstorm while the students work. Let them dip and mix the yarn into the paint. Take a piece of construction paper and fold it in half. Ask the child to lay each piece of yarn on the paper with a little bit hanging off the edge. When student has all pieces on the paper ask them to fold the paper and then pull one string at a time out which will leave streaks of rain when you open it up. These will all look very different. You may then provide students with white and black tempera paint and paintbrushes to create rain clouds and yellow for bolts of lightning. You can also provide cotton balls for clouds instead of paint.	Construction paper, yarn, white, blue, black, yellow tempera paint, paintbrushes	Assessment Photo
Cognitive Development Language Development Sensory Development Social/Emotional Dev. Fine Motor Development	**Question:** What is wind? Write all the children's responses on the board or chart paper. **View:** Use the internet to view soft winds and hard winds such as hurricanes. **STEM/STEAM PROJECT:** Windy Art. Provide student with a feather. Ask them to place the feather on the table and blow. Ask the students about what happened to the	Fan, feathers, blue paint, pencils with erasers, cardstock	Assessment Photo

feather when they blow on it and continue to ask questions about such things as what happens to the leaves outside when the wind blows. Next have the student hold their feather in front of a fan. Ask them what they think will happen when they let go of their feather. Then ask them to let go of their feather and observe the fan blow the feather into the air. Last, have the student finger paint a piece of cardstock blue (let them paint the whole paper). Then hand them a pencil (eraser-side) and ask them to draw what they observed the feather do when the fan blew it into the wet paint. Finally, after the student is finished demonstrating the movement of the feather, give the student the feather and let them place it on their painting for representation. You may also follow this project up with their own description of wind.

STANDARDS	TIME	CIRCLE TIME ACTIVITIES	MATERIALS	DOCUMENTATION
Cognitive Development Language Development Gross Motor Development Social/Emotional Dev.		CIRCLE TIME: 1. Calendar Activities (Days, Months, Counting, Patterns, Season, Year) - Have the students shake their hips from side-to-side as they count the days of the month	Calendar, colored calendar numbers, music source	Assessment Photo
Cognitive Development Language Development Social/Emotional Dev.		2. Music & Movement: Story Time: Books spring, flowers, plants, gardens, dirt, rain, wind, etc.		Assessment Photo

STANDARDS	TIME	EXTRA ACTIVITIES	MATERIALS	DOCUMENTATION

24. Relevant Writing 1

Name Recognition and Practice

_____

Letter Recognition and Practice

X_____

X_____

What is something that is little?

_____is little.

Sight word recognition and practice.

little _____

*Encourage student to draw a picture of something little on the next page.

24. Week 24 Shopping List

ITEMS	YES, we have this item	NO, we need to buy	$ COST Of item	ITEMS	YES, we have this item	NO, we need to buy	$ COST Of item
PROVOCATION: Cookie sheet straws				SENSORY: Water plastic/foam cups cotton balls			
small objects of different weights such as pom poms, pebble, cotton ball, paper clip, etc.				PROCESS ART: Construction paper yarn			
MORNING MEETING: Music device White-board chart paper sharpie dry-erase marker				White, blue, black, yellow tempera paint			
				Paint brushes			
WRITING: Highlighter chart paper Pencils				STEAM: Fan Feathers blue paint pencils w/ erasers cardstock			

24. Parent Letter

Dear Family,

The wind is blowing and the rain is falling at school! Your child will be immersed in the weather of the season this week! This is a great time to discuss why we need rain and the science behind storms, so they me seem a little less scary. You should also talk to your child about storm/tornado safety and where the safest place is in your house. You can also have a tornado drill at your own house.

Provocation: Wind Experiments	Sensory: Let it Rain!	Letter/Word Focus: Xx, Little
Process Art: Rainstorms	STEM Project: Windy Art	Writing: _____ is little.

DAILY SCHEDULE & PLANS

STANDARDS	TIME	DAILY ACTIVITIES	MATERIALS	DOCUMENTATION
Cognitive Development Language Development Fine Motor Development	------	**Weekly Transition:** Rhyming. Pick a word such as "cat" and have each child give you a word that rhymes with "cat". Silly words count, too!		Assessment
Cognitive Development Sensory Development	------	**Extension Center:**		Assessment Photo
Cognitive Development Language Development Gross Motor Development Sensory Development Social/Emotional Dev. Fine Motor Development		*What was successful and interesting to students last week? Carry this over to a center this week, so the students may extend this play/learning.* **Provocation:** Rainbows! Place several bowls or a tray with separate compartments in it on the table. Fill the bowls/compartments with a variety of tissue paper pieces (cut into 2'x2' squares or close to this) in all the colors of the rainbow that can be glued onto paper. Provide student with paper, glue and a paintbrush (for the glue) and let them create! Rainbow collage, rainbow monster, etc.!!	Construction paper or cardstock, glue, paintbrushes, multi-colored tissue paper squares, bowls	Assessment Photo
Cognitive Development Language Development Sensory Development Fine Motor Development		**Morning Meeting:** 1. Good morning song (Teacher's choice) 2. Monday: Morning Message **Letter/Word Focus:** Vv, play 3. Tues-Fri: **"My News"** **/Writing Prompt:** What do you like to play with? I play with _____.	Music device, white-board, chart paper, sharpie, dry-erase marker	Assessment Photo

STANDARDS	TIME	OUTDOOR ACTIVITIES	MATERIALS	DOCUMENTATION
Cognitive Development Language Development Sensory Development Fine Motor Development		**Outdoor time/Free Choice:**		Assessment Photo

Optional activities include: watering plants, pulling weeds, gardening, sensory, snow painting, snowman building, snow shoveling, raking leaves, etc.

Extra Activities:

STANDARDS	TIME	LEARNING CENTER ACTIVITY CHOICES	MATERIALS	DOCUMENTATION
Cognitive Development Language Development Fine Motor Development		**WRITING:** Name, Letter Focus, My News/Writing Prompt. Use relevant writing sheets to complete writing time or allow the students time to freely draw and the teacher to dictate the students' drawing. Teacher can use the dictation to encourage identification of letters and words along with independent writing.	Highlighter, pencils or crayons	Assessment Photo
Cognitive Development Sensory Development		**SENSORY:** Coin Dig! Fill the sensory bin with shaving cream. You can add a few drops of green watercolor paint or food coloring along with some green glitter. Let the student stir it up. Drop in gold coins or money coins (real or pretend). Stir and then let the student go dig for coins! This is an opportunity to teach the recognition and value of coins. Place 4 plates on the table for pennies, dimes, nickels and quarters. Place one of each coin on the corresponding plate and as the student digs out the coins have them place them on the appropriate plate. You may also place a value on each plate such as 1, 5, 10, and 25.	Shaving cream, green watercolor/food coloring, pretend/real coins, 4 plates, spoons	Assessment Photo
Cognitive Development Language Development Gross Motor Development		**Learning Centers:** *Note any changes and/or additions made to learning		Assessment Photo

Sensory Development
Social/Emotional Dev.
Fine Motor Development

centers

Cognitive Development
Language Development
Sensory Development
Fine Motor Development

PROCESS ART:
Leprechaun Gold! Provide the student with several rocks (finding the rocks can also be part of the activity) and gold paint. Let them explore painting the rocks gold. Let the rocks dry and place them in a bowl. You may also use a Sharpie to write the letters of the child's name or sight word on the rocks.

Rocks, gold paint, paintbrushes, bowl, Sharpie

Assessment
Photo

Cognitive Development
Language Development
Sensory Development
Social/Emotional Dev.
Fine Motor Development

Questions: Read a book about leprechauns and then provide the children with some information about Leprechauns and how they can be very mischievous (discuss the meaning of the word mischievous). Then let the children know that if a leprechaun decides to pull some shenanigans this week then we will try and catch him in the trap! Guide the children in a conversation about the trap. What color is the trap? What would lure the leprechaun in? How can we get the trap off the ground? What would cause the trap to fall onto the leprechaun?

Box, glue, pipe-cleaners, popsicle sticks, paint, any extra craft supplies you may have on hand, green paint

Assessment
Photo

View: Use the internet to view Leprechaun traps

STEAM: Leprechaun Trap! This is a group project. Provide a box (large or small) and supplies such as paint, glue, craft sticks, pipe-cleaners, cups, rubber bands, most any extra craft supplies you can find hanging around the art area. Begin to build the trap using the various supplies. To add to the excitement each morning you can mess up an area of the room and place a couple of green footprints near the shenanigans! Then check the trap to see if they caught the leprechaun!

STANDARDS	TIME	CIRCLE TIME ACTIVITIES	MATERIALS	DOCUMENTATION
Cognitive Development Language Development Gross Motor Development Social/Emotional Dev.		**CIRCLE TIME:** **1.** Calendar Activities (Days, Months, Counting, Season, Year) -Have the students jump while counting the days of the month	Calendar, colored calendar numbers, music source	Assessment Photo
Cognitive Development Language Development Social/Emotional Dev.		**2.** Music & Movement: **Story Time:** Books spring, flowers, plants, gardens, dirt, rain, St. Patrick's Day, rainbows, Leprechauns, Ireland, shamrocks		Assessment Photo

STANDARDS	TIME	EXTRA ACTIVITIES	MATERIALS	DOCUMENTATION

25. Relevant Writing 1

Name Recognition and Practice

_____

Letter Recognition and Practice

V_____

v_____

What do you like to play?

I play _____.

Sight word recognition and practice.

Play _____

*Encourage student to draw a picture of what they play on next page.

25. Week 25 Shopping List

ITEMS	YES, we have this item	NO, we need to buy	$ COST Of item	ITEMS	YES, we have this item	NO, we need to buy	$ COST Of item
PROVOCATION: Construction paper/ cardstock Glue Paintbrushes				**SENSORY:** Shaving cream green watercolor/food coloring pretend/real coins 4 plates spoons			
multi-colored tissue paper squares				**PROCESS ART:** Rocks gold paint paintbrushes Bowl Sharpie			
bowls				**STEAM:** Box Glue Pipe-cleaners popsicle sticks Paint any extra craft supplies you may have on hand green paint			
MORNING MEETING: Music device White-board chart paper sharpie dry-erase marker							
WRITING: Highlighter chart paper Pencils							

25. Parent Letter

Dear Family,

Happy St. Patrick's Day! This is a great week to point out the color green and expand your child's cultural knowledge. You can search the internet for stories about leprechauns, shamrocks, and of course the "pot of gold" at the end of the rainbow! This is also a great time to introduce your child to geography. You can use a globe, map or the internet to show your child where you live and where the country of Ireland is. Show your child pictures of Ireland and possibly check out a book at the library about Ireland.

Provocation: Rainbows	Sensory: Find the coins	Letter/Word Focus: Yy, Play
Process Art: Making Gold	STEM Project: Leprechaun Trap	Writing: I play_____

DAILY SCHEDULE & PLANS

STANDARDS	TIME	DAILY ACTIVITIES	MATERIALS	DOCUMENTATION
Cognitive Development Language Development Fine Motor Development	------	**Weekly Transition:** Birth month. Ask the students, "If you were born in the month of _____ then you may………. (line up, wash your hands, etc.,)"	Keep a list of birthdays nearby for easy access	Assessment
Cognitive Development Sensory Development	------	**Extension Center:**		Assessment Photo
Cognitive Development Language Development Gross Motor Development Sensory Development Social/Emotional Dev. Fine Motor Development		*What was successful and interesting to students last week? Carry this over to a center this week, so the students may extend this play/learning.* **Provocation:** The Fine Motor Egg Cartons. Provide egg cartons and tongs/tweezers along with several bowls of small objects (rocks, corks, bottle caps, buttons, etc.) that can be lifted by tweezers into the carton holes. You may also label the holes with numbers and ask the student to provide a certain number of objects or you may just let them explore and work on their fine motor skills.	Egg cartons, tongs/tweezers, bowls with small objects	Assessment Photo
Cognitive Development Language Development Sensory Development Fine Motor Development		**Morning Meeting:** 1. Good morning song (Teacher's choice) 2. Monday: Morning Message **Letter/Word Focus:** Zz, make 3. Tues-Fri: "**My News**"/**Writing Prompt:** I can make a _____.	Music device, white-board, chart paper, sharpie, dry-erase marker	Assessment Photo

STANDARDS	TIME	OUTDOOR ACTIVITIES	MATERIALS	DOCUMENTATION
Cognitive Development Language Development Sensory Development Fine Motor Development		Outdoor time/Free Choice:		Assessment Photo

Optional activities include:

watering plants, pulling weeds,
gardening, sensory, snow
painting, snowman building,
snow shoveling, raking leaves,
etc.

Extra Activities:

STANDARDS	TIME	LEARNING CENTER ACTIVITY CHOICES	MATERIALS	DOCUMENTATION
Cognitive Development Language Development Fine Motor Development		**WRITING:** Name, Letter Focus, My News/Writing Prompt. Use relevant writing sheets to complete writing time or allow the students time to freely draw and the teacher to dictate the students' drawing. Teacher can use the dictation to encourage identification of letters and words along with independent writing.	Highlighter, pencils or crayons	Assessment Photo
Cognitive Development Sensory Development		**SENSORY:** Bird Seed! Fill the sensory bin with bird seed, a few plastic eggs, and a few pretend birds (rubber ducks will work) and let the students explore. You may also add a couple of measuring cups and a funnel.	Bird seed, plastic eggs, pretend birds, measuring cups,, funnel	Assessment Photo
Cognitive Development Language Development Gross Motor Development Sensory Development Social/Emotional Dev. Fine Motor Development		**Learning Centers:** *Note any changes and/or additions made to learning centers*		Assessment Photo
Cognitive Development Language Development Sensory Development Fine Motor Development		**PROCESS ART:** Feather painting! Set the table with several colors of paint and feathers for painting. Provide the student with a piece of construction paper and ask them to use the feathers as	Feathers, paint, construction paper	Assessment Photo

STANDARDS	TIME	ACTIVITIES	MATERIALS	DOCUMENTATION
Cognitive Development Language Development Sensory Development Social/Emotional Dev. Fine Motor Development		paint brushes. Let them create! **Question:** What does a bird use to build a nest? As the students answer make a list on the board/chart paper. **View:** Use the internet to view a time lapse of a bird making a nest. **STEAM:** Build a nest! Provide a tray or several bowls with a variety of materials such as shredded paper, pipe-cleaners, yarn pieces, fabric pieces, fake grass (raffia), strips of newspaper, and some plastic eggs. You can let the students begin building or you can provide them a small bowl to begin their nest. When they are finished you may ask them what the bird would look like. You can dictate this onto a piece of paper to attach to the nest for display. They may also want to draw the bird.	Shredded paper, pipe-cleaners, yarn pieces, fabric pieces, fake grass, plastic eggs, Styrofoam bowls, paper for dictation	Assessment Photo

STANDARDS	TIME	CIRCLE TIME ACTIVITIES	MATERIALS	DOCUMENTATION
Cognitive Development Language Development Gross Motor Development Social/Emotional Dev.		**CIRCLE TIME:** 1. Calendar Activities (Days, Months, Counting, Number Recognition, Season, Year) -Do jumping jacks while counting the days in the month -Cheer the letters in the month (i.e. Give me a M, A, R, C, H...what does that spell?)	Calendar, colored calendar numbers, music source	Assessment Photo
Cognitive Development Language Development Social/Emotional Dev.		2. Music & Movement: **Story Time:** Books about spring, birds, nests, etc.		Assessment Photo

26. Relevant Writing 1

Name Recognition and Practice

_____

Letter Recognition and Practice

Z_____

z_____

What can you make with your hands?

I can make a _____.

Sight word recognition and practice.

Make_____

*Encourage student to draw a picture of what you can make on the next page.

26. Week 26 Shopping List

ITEMS	YES, we have this item	NO, we need to buy	$ COST Of item	ITEMS	YES, we have this item	NO, we need to buy	$ COST Of item
PROVOCATION: Egg cartons tongs/tweezers bowls with small objects				**SENSORY:** Bird seed plastic eggs pretend birds containers funnel			
MORNING MEETING: Music device Whiteboard chart paper sharpie dry-erase marker				**PROCESS ART:** Feathers paint construction paper			
WRITING: Highlighter chart paper Pencils				**STEAM:** Shredded paper pipe-cleaners yarn pieces fabric pieces fake grass plastic eggs Styrofoam bowls paper for dictation			

26. Parent Letter

Dear Family,

Let's talk about birds! This week you child will explore what birds eat, bird nests, and the look and feel of feathers. You can go on a bird search with your child. Explore the colors of different birds, listen for the different bird calls, and maybe even discover a nest! Be sure to ask your child about the nest they created at school.

Provocation: The Fine Motor Egg Carton	Sensory: Bird Seed!	Letter/Word Focus: Vv, Make
Process Art: Feather Painting!	STEM Project: Build a Nest!	Writing: I can make a _____.

DAILY SCHEDULE & PLANS

STANDARDS	TIME	DAILY ACTIVITIES	MATERIALS	DOCUMENTATION
Cognitive Development Language Development Fine Motor Development	------	**Weekly Transition:** Sight word recognition. Write the sight words on an index card. Only Choose 3-5 for the week to practice. Ask the student to identify the sight word before transitioning.	Index cards, sharpie	Assessment
Cognitive Development Sensory Development	------	**Extension Center:**		Assessment Photo
		*What was successful and interesting to students last week? Carry this over to a center this week, so the students may extend this play/learning.		
Cognitive Development Language Development Gross Motor Development Sensory Development Social/Emotional Dev. Fine Motor Development		**Provocation:** Caterpillar Playdough. Set out some homemade playdough, a picture of a caterpillar and a few cut pieces of pipe cleaners for antennas and let them enjoy building and re-creating their own caterpillars	Homemade playdough, caterpillar picture/book, pipe cleaners	Assessment Photo
Cognitive Development Language Development Sensory Development Fine Motor Development		**Morning Meeting:** 1. Good morning song (Teacher's choice) 2. Monday: Morning Message **Letter/Word Focus:** Review A, B, & C/ Red 3. Tues-Fri: **"My News"** /Writing Prompt: _____ is red.	Music device, white-board, chart paper, sharpie, dry-erase marker	Assessment Photo

STANDARDS	TIME	OUTDOOR ACTIVITIES	MATERIALS	DOCUMENTATION
Cognitive Development Language Development Sensory Development Fine Motor Development		**Outdoor time/Free Choice:**		Assessment Photo

Optional activities include:

watering plants, pulling weeds, gardening, sensory, snow painting, snowman building, snow shoveling, raking leaves, etc.

Extra Activities:

STANDARDS	TIME	LEARNING CENTER ACTIVITY CHOICES	MATERIALS	DOCUMENTATION
Cognitive Development Language Development Fine Motor Development		**WRITING:** Name, Letter Focus, My News/Writing Prompt. Use relevant writing sheets to complete writing time or allow the students time to freely draw and the teacher to dictate the students' drawing. Teacher can use the dictation to encourage identification of letters and words along with independent writing.	Highlighter, pencils or crayons	Assessment Photo
Cognitive Development Sensory Development		**SENSORY:** The Flower Garden! Fill the sensory bin with organic potting soil and a few rocks (optional: this could be a swallowing hazard). Then provide small shovels, buckets, plastic worms, and silk flowers for pretend planting.	Silk flowers, plastic worms, potting soil, bucket, shovel	Assessment Photo
Cognitive Development Language Development Gross Motor Development Sensory Development Social/Emotional Dev. Fine Motor Development		**Learning Centers:** *Note any changes and/or additions made to learning centers*		Assessment Photo

Cognitive Development Language Development Sensory Development Fine Motor Development	PROCESS ART: Butterfly Symmetry! Use a book or the internet to discuss and observe the parts of a butterfly. Using a Sharpie draw ½ of butterfly for your students and then ask them what the other ½ would look like. Provide students a paper with ½ of a butterfly. Provide them a Sharpie to draw the other ½. Encourage detail and design. Last provide the student with watercolors to paint the butterfly.	Construction paper, Sharpies/markers, Butterfly book or Internet, watercolors	Assessment Photo
Cognitive Development Language Development Sensory Development Social/Emotional Dev. Fine Motor Development	Question: What do you think it would feel like to be in a chrysalis?

View: Use the internet to view the life cycle of a butterfly and also view a time lapse of a caterpillar creating a chrysalis

STEAM: Life Cycle of a Butterfly? Talk about the different stages of the butterfly. Use a bean to represent the tiny egg, then use a piece of yarn to present the caterpillar, use a pasta shell to represent the chrysalis, and finally use a coffee filter and pipe cleaner (wrap pipe cleaner around the center of the coffee filter to create a body and 2 wings) to represent the butterfly. Ask if the students would like to feel what it's like to be in the chrysalis. Wrap the volunteers in toilet paper to resemble the chrysalis! This should be very entertaining. Allow them to wrap each other. When they are finished with the activity offer them the opportunity to create their own butterfly life cycle to take home. Provide a stick, bean, yarn, pasta shell and coffee filter butterfly. The student can decorate the coffee filter with markers and then glue the bean, yarn, pasta, and butterfly onto the stick in the life cycle order. | Toilet paper, beans, sticks, yarn pieces, pasta shells, markers, pipe cleaners, coffee filters | Assessment Photo |

The students can use a larger
piece of yarn to wrap around
the pasta and the stick to
model a caterpillar creating a
chrysalis.

STANDARDS	TIME	CIRCLE TIME ACTIVITIES	MATERIALS	DOCUMENTATION
Cognitive Development Language Development Gross Motor Development Social/Emotional Dev.		**CIRCLE TIME:** **1.** Calendar Activities (Days, Months, Counting, Number Recognition, Season, Year) -Do kicks while counting the days in the month -Cheer the letters in the Days of the week (i.e. Give me a M, O, N, D, A, Y...what does that spell?)	Calendar, colored calendar numbers, music source	Assessment Photo
Cognitive Development Language Development Social/Emotional Dev.		**2.** Music & Movement: **Story Time:** Books about spring, butterflies, caterpillars, etc.		

STANDARDS	TIME	EXTRA ACTIVITIES	MATERIALS	DOCUMENTATION

Name Recognition and Practice

_____

Number Recognition and Practice

1_____

Letter Review

A_____

B_____

C_____

Can you think of something RED?

_____ is red.

Sight word recognition and practice.

Red_____

*Encourage student to draw a picture of something red on the next page.

27. Week 27 Shopping List

ITEMS	YES, we have this item	NO, we need to buy	$ COST Of item	ITEMS	YES, we have this item	NO, we need to buy	$ COST Of item
PROVOCATION: Homemade playdough caterpillar picture/book pipe cleaners				SENSORY: Silk flowers plastic worms potting soil bucket shovel			
MORNING MEETING: Music device White-board chart paper sharpie dry-erase marker				PROCESS ART: Construction paper Sharpies Butterfly book or Internet watercolors			
WRITING: Highlighter chart paper Pencils				STEAM: Toilet paper beans sticks yarn pieces pasta shells markers pipe cleaners coffee filters			

27. Parent Letter

Dear Family,

Flowers, caterpillars and butterflies! This week your child will dig in the flower garden, create caterpillars, and learn about the life cycle of a butterfly. The most fun activity will be getting inside a chrysalis! Explore nature with your child by planting flowers and/or looking for butterflies.

Provocation: Playdough Caterpillars!	Sensory: The Flower Garden!	Letter/Word Focus: Review A, B, C / Red
Process Art: Butterfly Symmetry!	STEM Project: Life Cycle of a Butterfly	Writing: _____ is red.

DAILY SCHEDULE & PLANS

STANDARDS	TIME	DAILY ACTIVITIES	MATERIALS	DOCUMENTATION
Cognitive Development Language Development Fine Motor Development	------	**Weekly Transition:** Sight word recognition. Write the sight words on an index card. Only Choose 3-5 for the week to practice. Ask the student to identify the sight word before transitioning.	Index cards, sharpie	Assessment
Cognitive Development Sensory Development	------	**Extension Center:**		Assessment Photo
Cognitive Development Language Development Gross Motor Development Sensory Development Social/Emotional Dev. Fine Motor Development		*What was successful and interesting to students last week? Carry this over to a center this week, so the students may extend this play/learning.* **Provocation:** Egg Decorating Station! Place construction paper/cardstock cut into the shape of an egg on a table. Provide bowls or a divided tray with a variety of decorating items such as hole-punched circles, buttons, paper strips, tissue pieces, and glue for attaching the pieces to the egg. You can also change this up throughout the week to a variety of paint colors. Design one or two eggs to demonstrate the possibilities then let the students explore and create.	Construction paper, a variety of items such as hole-punched paper, paper strips, buttons, etc., glue, paint	Assessment Photo
Cognitive Development Language Development Sensory Development Fine Motor Development		**Morning Meeting:** 1. Good morning song (Teacher's choice) 2. Monday: Morning Message **Letter/Word Focus:** Review D, E, F / Blue 3. Tues-Fri: **"My News"** **/Writing Prompt:** _____ is blue.	Music device, white-board, chart paper, sharpie, dry-erase marker	Assessment Photo

STANDARDS	TIME	OUTDOOR ACTIVITIES	MATERIALS	DOCUMENTATION
Cognitive Development Language Development Sensory Development Fine Motor Development		Outdoor time/Free Choice: *Optional activities include: watering plants, pulling weeds, gardening, sensory, snow painting, snowman building, snow shoveling, raking leaves, etc.* **Extra Activities:**		Assessment Photo

STANDARDS	TIME	LEARNING CENTER ACTIVITY CHOICES	MATERIALS	DOCUMENTATION
Cognitive Development Language Development Fine Motor Development		**WRITING:** Name, Letter Focus, My News/Writing Prompt. Use relevant writing sheets to complete writing time or allow the students time to freely draw and the teacher to dictate the students' drawing. Teacher can use the dictation to encourage identification of letters and words along with independent writing.	Highlighter, pencils or crayons	Assessment Photo
Cognitive Development Sensory Development		**SENSORY:** Water Bead Eggs! Fill the sensory bin with a small amount of water (about an inch or two) and poor in some water beads. Add plastic eggs to the bin and let the children explore filling the eggs with the beads. Great sensory and fine motor activity. Add measuring spoons and cups throughout the week.	Water, water beads, plastic eggs	Assessment Photo
Cognitive Development Language Development Gross Motor Development Sensory Development Social/Emotional Dev. Fine Motor Development		**Learning Centers:** *Note any changes and/or additions made to learning centers*		Assessment Photo

Cognitive Development Language Development Sensory Development Fine Motor Development	**PROCESS ART:** Egg Drip Painting! This can be a group project completed on a large piece of butcher paper. Roll the paper onto the floor and tape down the edges. Provide several different colors of paint in cups. You will need to water down the tempera paint so it will flow easily through the hole in the plastic eggs. Next, provide plastic eggs with holes (check before you buy or create the hole yourself). Last, allow the child to pour or dip the egg half into the paint to fill the egg and then drip the paint onto the paper. You can demonstrate different ways to drip such as in a circular motion or zigzag motion.	Butcher paper, tape, plastic eggs with holes, tempera paint	Assessment Photo
Cognitive Development Language Development Sensory Development Social/Emotional Dev. Fine Motor Development	**Question:** Why doesn't the egg break when the chicken sits on it? **View:** Use the internet to view chickens sitting on eggs. **STEAM:** You will need 4-6 dozen eggs for this experiment. The first step is to ask a student to open their hand, place the egg in the palm of their hand and then ask them to close their hand around the egg (like making a fist) to demonstrate that the egg while not break when applying pressure. Now ask a student to use the tips of their fingers to squeeze the egg to show the egg breaking. Why? The dome-shaped design distributes pressure evenly. Now open 4-6 dozen egg cartons, make sure all the	4-6 dozen eggs in cartons	Assessment Photo

eggs are turned the same way, place the cartons within stepping distance of each other, have students take of their shoes and socks, help the student to step onto the first carton of eggs (evenly) and hold their hand to walk across the other cartons. WOW! They don't break! Talk about the structure of the egg and why it doesn't break.

* Make sure children wash hands thoroughly with soap and water after having contact with the inside of an egg.

STANDARDS	TIME	CIRCLE TIME ACTIVITIES	MATERIALS	DOCUMENTATION
Cognitive Development Language Development Gross Motor Development Social/Emotional Dev.		**CIRCLE TIME:** **1.** Calendar Activities (Days, Months, Counting, Number Recognition, Season, Year) -Hop on one foot while counting the days in the month -Count the days of the month backwards	Calendar, colored calendar numbers, music source	Assessment Photo
Cognitive Development Language Development Social/Emotional Dev.		**2.** Music & Movement: **Story Time:** Books about spring, baby chicks, eggs, rabbits, farm animals, etc.		Assessment Photo

28. Relevant Writing 1

Name Recognition and Practice

_____

Number Recognition and Practice

1_____ **2**_____

Letter Review

D_____

E_____

F_____

Can you think of something blue?

_____ **is** blue

Sight word recognition and practice.

Blue_____

*Encourage student to draw a picture of something blue on the next page.

28. Week 28 Shopping List

ITEMS	YES, we have this item	NO, we need to buy	$ COST Of item	ITEMS	YES, we have this item	NO, we need to buy	$ COST Of item
PROVOCATION: Construction paper a variety of items such as hole-punched paper, paper strips, buttons, etc. Glue paint				SENSORY: Water water beads plastic eggs			
MORNING MEETING: Music device White-board chart paper sharpie dry-erase marker				PROCESS ART: Butcher paper tape plastic eggs with holes tempera paint			
WRITING: Highlighter chart paper Pencils				STEAM: 4-6 dozen eggs in cartons			

28. Parent Letter

Dear Family,

This week we will be talking about eggs and baby chicks. We will explore the question, "Why doesn't an egg break when the chicken sits on it?" This is a great time of year to discuss baby animals or take a field trip to a farm. You may even be able to take a field trip to your local farm store to see some real live baby chicks and/or rabbits!

Provocation: Egg Decorating!	Sensory: Water Beads & Eggs!	Letter/Word Focus: Review D, E, F / Blue
Process Art: Egg Drip Painting!	STEM Project: Why doesn't an egg break when the chicken sits on it?	Writing: _____ is blue.

DATE: _____ WEEK #:_29_ TITLE: _Dinosaurs__ TEACHER: _____

DAILY SCHEDULE & PLANS

STANDARDS	TIME	DAILY ACTIVITIES	MATERIALS	DOCUMENTATION
Cognitive Development Language Development Fine Motor Development	------	**Weekly Transition:** Number recognition. Write numbers 1-30 on an index card. Only Choose 3-5 for the week to practice. Ask the student to identify the number before transitioning. *You may also use this time to choose 2 numbers for students to add together depending on where the students are.	Index cards, sharpie	Assessment
Cognitive Development Sensory Development	------	**Extension Center** *What was successful and interesting to students last week? Carry this over to a center this week, so the students may extend this play/learning.*		Assessment Photo
Cognitive Development Language Development Gross Motor Development Sensory Development Social/Emotional Dev. Fine Motor Development		**Provocation:** Little Dinosaur Worlds. Begin with some type of shallow container such as cookie sheet/casserole dish/shallow bowl/flower pot and add sand, a few rocks, a few tree trimmings, sticks and miniature to small dinosaurs (depending on the size of your container to create a small dinosaur sanctuary that students can explore and play with on a tabletop. You may want to create 2-4 depending on the number of students. Also, you may add a small bowl of water inside the sanctuary for a dinosaur watering hole!	Shallow container, sticks, rocks, sand, tree trimmings, small dinosaurs	Assessment Photo
Cognitive Development Language Development Sensory Development Fine Motor Development		**Morning Meeting:** 1. Good morning song (Teacher's choice) 2. Monday: Morning Message **Letter/Word Focus:** Review G, H, I/ Yellow 3. Tues-Fri: **"My News"** /Writing Prompt: _____ is yellow.	Music device, white-board, chart paper, sharpie, dry-erase marker	Assessment Photo

234

STANDARDS	TIME	OUTDOOR ACTIVITIES	MATERIALS	DOCUMENTATION
Cognitive Development Language Development Sensory Development Fine Motor Development		Outdoor time/Free Choice:		Assessment Photo
		Optional activities include: watering plants, pulling weeds, gardening, sensory, snow painting, snowman building, snow shoveling, raking leaves, etc. **Extra Activities:**		

STANDARDS	TIME	LEARNING CENTER ACTIVITY CHOICES	MATERIALS	DOCUMENTATION
Cognitive Development Language Development Fine Motor Development		**WRITING:** Name, Letter Focus, My News/Writing Prompt. Use relevant writing sheets to complete writing time or allow the students time to freely draw and the teacher to dictate the students' drawing. Teacher can use the dictation to encourage identification of letters and words along with independent writing.	Highlighter, pencils or crayons	Assessment Photo
Cognitive Development Sensory Development		**SENSORY:** Hatching Dinosaur Eggs! Blow up several balloons (depending on how many eggs you want to place in your sensory bin) and let the air out to stretch the balloons. Place a miniature dinosaur inside each balloon. Fill the balloon (to the size you want the eggs) with water, tie, and place in freezer. Add a bowl of warm water and some syringes to the bin, so students can melt the eggs and retrieve the dinosaurs!	Water, miniature dinosaurs, balloons, syringes, bowl	Assessment Photo
Cognitive Development Language Development Gross Motor Development Sensory Development Social/Emotional Dev.		**Learning Centers:** *Note any changes and/or additions made to learning centers*		Assessment Photo

235

Cognitive Development Language Development Sensory Development Fine Motor Development	**PROCESS ART:** Team Building Dinosaurs. Using poster board cut out large silhouettes of dinosaurs. Cut a variety of different shapes and sizes from multi-colored construction paper. Provide a bowl with glue and paint brushes, so the students can easily create their own unique dinosaurs. Allow the children to work in teams to cover the dinosaur silhouettes.	Poster board, multi-color construction paper, glue, bowl, paintbrushes, scissors	Assessment Photo
Cognitive Development Language Development Sensory Development Social/Emotional Dev. Fine Motor Development	**Question of the Day:** How do we know there were dinosaurs on the Earth? **View:** Use the internet to view dinosaur fossils and paleontologist digging up dinosaur bones **STEAM:** Dinosaur Excavation! First, create Ooblek by mixing 1 cup water to 1 cup cornstarch (may have to add cornstarch if too wet or water if too dry). Place small dinosaurs or dinosaur bones into plastic dish/plastic bowls/Styrofoam bowls and cover with Ooblek mixture. Let sit in a sunny place for a couple of days to dry. Give the students their bowl and a tool such as a spoon or unsharpened pencil and ask them to become archeologist and carefully dig for their dinosaur or dinosaur bones.	Water, cornstarch, miniature dinosaurs or plastic dinosaur bones, styrofoam bowls/plastic dishes, spoons/unsharpened pencils	Assessment Photo

STANDARDS	TIME	CIRCLE TIME ACTIVITIES	MATERIALS	DOCUMENTATION
Cognitive Development Language Development Gross Motor Development Social/Emotional Dev.		**CIRCLE TIME:** **1.** Calendar Activities (Days, Months, Counting, Number Recognition, Patterns, Season, Year) -Do push-ups while counting the days in the month -Incorporate exercise and counting by 10's such as count by 10's while doing jumping jacks. **2.** Music & Movement:	Calendar, colored calendar numbers, music source	Assessment Photo
Cognitive Development Language Development Social/Emotional Dev.		**Story Time:** Books about Dinosaurs and fossils		Assessment Photo

STANDARDS	TIME	EXTRA ACTIVITIES	MATERIALS	DOCUMENTATION

29. Relevant Writing 1

Name Recognition and Practice

_____

Number Recognition and Practice

1_____ **2**_____ **3**_____

Letter Review and Practice

G_____ **H**_____

I_____

29. Relevant Writing 2

Can you think of something yellow?

_____ is yellow.

Sight word recognition and practice.

Yellow_____

*Encourage student to draw a picture of something yellow on the next page.

29. Week 29 Shopping List

ITEMS	YES, we have this item	NO, we need to buy	$ COST Of item	ITEMS	YES, we have this item	NO, we need to buy	$ COST Of item
PROVOCATION: Shallow container sticks rocks Sand tree trimmings small dinosaurs				**SENSORY:** Water miniature dinosaurs balloons syringes bowl **PROCESS ART:** Poster board multi-color construction paper glue bowl Paint brushes scissors			
MORNING MEETING: Music device White-board chart paper sharpie dry-erase marker				**STEAM:** Water Cornstarch miniature dinosaurs or plastic dinosaur bones Styrofoam bowls/plastic dishes, spoons/ unsharpened pencils			
WRITING: Highlighter chart paper Pencils							

29. Parent Letter

Dear Family,

This week we will be talking about Dinosaurs. We will explore the question, "How do we know dinosaurs existed and what is a paleontologist?" Dinosaurs is a popular topic among many preschoolers and this is also a perfect time for your family to visit a science museum or dinosaur exhibit. Your child will be amazed and in wonder at the size of these creatures.

Provocation: Little Dino Worlds!	Sensory: Hatching Dinosaur Eggs!	Letter/Word Focus: Review G, H, I / Yellow
Process Art: Team Building Dinosaurs!	STEM Project: Dinosaur Excavation!	Writing: _____ is yellow.

DATE: _____ WEEK #:_30_ TITLE: _Boats, Trains, & Planes_ TEACHER:_____

DAILY SCHEDULE & PLANS

STANDARDS	TIME	DAILY ACTIVITIES	MATERIALS	DOCUMENTATION
Cognitive Development Language Development Fine Motor Development	------	**Weekly Transition:** Continue sight word recognition. Write the sight words on an index card. Only Choose 3-5 for the week to practice. Ask the student to identify the sight word before transitioning.	Index cards, sharpie	Assessment
Cognitive Development Sensory Development	------	*You can mix this up with letter recognition cards **Extension Center:**		Assessment Photo
Cognitive Development Language Development Gross Motor Development Sensory Development Social/Emotional Dev. Fine Motor Development		*What was successful and interesting to students last week? Carry this over to a center this week, so the students may extend this play/learning. **Provocation:** Train Tracks! Lay out a long piece of butcher paper on the table. Tape both end of the paper so it will not move. Using a black Sharpie, draw a long train track across the bottom. Place crayons on the table and ask the students to add to the train track picture.	Butcher paper, crayons, Sharpie	Assessment Photo
Cognitive Development Language Development Sensory Development Fine Motor Development		**Morning Meeting:** 1. Good morning song (Teacher's choice) 2. Monday: Morning Message **Letter/Word Focus:** Review J, K, L/green 3. Tues-Fri: "My News" /Writing Prompt: _____ is green.	Music device, white-board, chart paper, sharpie, dry-erase marker	Assessment Photo

STANDARDS	TIME	OUTDOOR ACTIVITIES	MATERIALS	DOCUMENTATION
Cognitive Development Language Development Sensory Development Fine Motor Development		**Outdoor time/Free Choice:**		Assessment Photo

243

Optional activities include: watering plants, pulling weeds, gardening, sensory, snow painting, snowman building, snow shoveling, raking leaves, etc.

Extra Activities:

STANDARDS	TIME	LEARNING CENTER ACTIVITY CHOICES	MATERIALS	DOCUMENTATION
Cognitive Development Language Development Fine Motor Development		**WRITING:** Name, Letter Focus, My News/Writing Prompt. Use relevant writing sheets to complete writing time or allow the students time to freely draw and the teacher to dictate the students' drawing. Teacher can use the dictation to encourage identification of letters and words along with independent writing.	Highlighter, pencils or crayons	Assessment Photo
Cognitive Development Sensory Development		**SENSORY:** Shaving Cream Car Wash! Use two sensory tubs. Spray shaving cream in one tub and place water in the other tub. Provide toy cars, trucks, planes, trains and allow the students to explore soaping the vehicles with shaving cream, cleaning them with water, and drying them with a towel.	Water, shaving cream, towels, toy vehicles	Assessment Photo
Cognitive Development Language Development Gross Motor Development Sensory Development Social/Emotional Dev. Fine Motor Development		**Learning Centers:** *Note any changes and/or additions made to learning centers*		Assessment Photo
Cognitive Development		**PROCESS ART:** Train	Trains, paint, plates,	Assessment

244

STANDARDS	TIME	ACTIVITIES	MATERIALS	DOCUMENTATION
Language Development Sensory Development Fine Motor Development		Painting. Place several small plates on the table. Pour washable paint on each plate and set a train/car on top of the paint. Provide each student with a piece of construction paper and let them explore painting with the trains/cars! The students will roll their car through the paint and roll the car onto their paper.	construction paper	Photo
Cognitive Development Language Development Sensory Development Social/Emotional Dev. Fine Motor Development		**Question of the Day:** Why doesn't the boat sink? **View:** Use the internet to view a picture or video of a boat on the water **STEAM:** Using a piece of aluminum foil, shape it into a boat or raft and place it into a sensory bin with water for the students to see it floating. Now ask them what might happen if you place pennies in the boat. Let students help to place one penny at a time (count the pennies) in the boat until it sinks. Finally give each student their own piece of aluminum foil to build a boat. Create a boat challenge to see which boats float and which boat will hold the most pennies. You can also create a graph with the number of pennies it takes to sink the boat. Then you can talk about who's boat held the most pennies and who's boat held the least amount. *Pennies can be a choking hazard	Sensory bin, aluminum foil, pennies, water	Assessment Photo

STANDARDS	TIME	CIRCLE TIME ACTIVITIES	MATERIALS	DOCUMENTATION
Cognitive Development Language Development Gross Motor Development Social/Emotional Dev.		**CIRCLE TIME:** 1. Calendar Activities (Days, Months, Counting, Number Recognition, Patterns, Season, Year) -Do knee lifts while counting the days in the month	Calendar, colored calendar numbers, music source	Assessment Photo

-Incorporate exercise and counting by 10's such as count by 10's while leaping forward then backwards.

2. Music & Movement
Recommended:
Story Time: Books about boats, trains, planes, trucks, etc.

Cognitive Development
Language Development
Social/Emotional Dev.

Assessment
Photo

STANDARDS	TIME	EXTRA ACTIVITIES	MATERIALS	DOCUMENTATION

30. Relevant Writing 1

Name Recognition and Practice

_____

Number Recognition and Practice

1_____ **2**_____ **3**_____

4_____ **5**_____ **6**_____

Letter Review and Practice

J_____ **K**_____

L_____

Can you think of something green?

_____ is green

Sight word recognition and practice.

Green_____

*Encourage student to draw a picture of something green on the next page.

30. Week 30 Shopping List

ITEMS	YES, we have this item	NO, we need to buy	$ COST Of item	ITEMS	YES, we have this item	NO, we need to buy	$ COST Of item
PROVOCATION: Butcher paper Crayons Sharpie				SENSORY: Water shaving cream Towels toy vehicles			
MORNING MEETING: Music device White-board chart paper sharpie dry-erase marker				PROCESS ART: Trains Paint Plates construction paper			
WRITING: Highlighter chart paper Pencils				STEAM: Sensory bin aluminum foil Pennies water			

30. Parent Letter

Dear Family,

This week we will be talking about planes, trains, and boats. We will explore the question, "Why does a boat float?" Students will use aluminum foil to create their own boats and then test them in water to see if they will float!

Provocation: The Train Track	Sensory: Car Wash!	Letter/Word Focus: Review J, K, L / Green
Process Art: Train Painting!	STEM Project: Build a Boat!	Writing: _____ is green.

DAILY SCHEDULE & PLANS

STANDARDS	TIME	DAILY ACTIVITIES	MATERIALS	DOCUMENTATION
Cognitive Development Language Development Fine Motor Development	-------	**Weekly Transition:** Number recognition. Write numbers 1-30 on an index card. Only Choose 3-5 for the week to practice. Ask the student to identify the number before transitioning. *You may also use this time to choose 2 numbers for students to add together depending on where the students are.	Index cards, sharpie	Assessment
Cognitive Development Sensory Development	-------	**Extension Center:**		Assessment Photo
Cognitive Development Language Development Gross Motor Development Sensory Development Social/Emotional Dev. Fine Motor Development		*What was successful and interesting to students last week? Carry this over to a center this week, so the students may extend this play/learning.* **Provocation:** Herbal Playdough. Make plain homemade playdough. Set the table with several fresh herbs in bowls. Allow the students to experiment with touching and smelling the herbs and then adding the herbs to their playdough.	Homemade playdough, fresh herbs	Assessment Photo
Cognitive Development Language Development Sensory Development Fine Motor Development		**Morning Meeting:** 1. Good morning song (Teacher's choice) 2. Monday: Morning Message **Letter/Word Focus:** Review M, N, O; Black 3. Tues-Fri: **"My News"** /**Writing Prompt:** _____ is black.	Music device, white-board, chart paper, sharpie, dry-erase marker	Assessment Photo

STANDARDS	TIME	OUTDOOR ACTIVITIES	MATERIALS	DOCUMENTATION
Cognitive Development Language Development Sensory Development Fine Motor Development		Outdoor time/Free Choice: *Optional activities include: watering plants, pulling weeds, gardening, sensory, snow painting, snowman building, snow shoveling, raking leaves, etc.* **Extra Activities:**		Assessment Photo

STANDARDS	TIME	LEARNING CENTER ACTIVITY CHOICES	MATERIALS	DOCUMENTATION
Cognitive Development Language Development Fine Motor Development		**WRITING:** Name, Letter Focus, My News/Writing Prompt. Use relevant writing sheets to complete writing time or allow the students time to freely draw and the teacher to dictate the students' drawing. Teacher can use the dictation to encourage identification of letters and words along with independent writing.	Highlighter, pencils or crayons	Assessment Photo
Cognitive Development Sensory Development		**SENSORY:** Fairy Soup! Set out the sensory bin. Provide water, cut oranges or another citrus fruit, a little bit of water color (for coloring the water), rose petals, blades of grass, etc. along with a few wooden spoons. Then let them use their imagination to create a magical soup!	Water, watercolor, rose petals, cut oranges, blades of grass, wooden spoons	Assessment Photo
Cognitive Development Language Development Gross Motor Development Sensory Development Social/Emotional Dev. Fine Motor Development		Learning Centers: *Note any changes and/or additions made to learning centers*		Assessment Photo

Cognitive Development Language Development Sensory Development Fine Motor Development	**PROCESS ART:** Vegetable Printmaking! Provide a variety of cut vegetables such as a sliced bell pepper, a cut celery, carrot, potato and broccoli. Then set out a few plates with paint. Let the students dip the ends of the veggies in the paint and then stamp onto their construction paper to create a work of art	Cut vegetables, paint, plates, construction paper	Assessment Photo
Cognitive Development Language Development Sensory Development Social/Emotional Dev. Fine Motor Development	**Question of the Day:** What is a seed? **View:** Use the internet to view pictures or videos of different types of seeds. You can also bring in several different types of seeds that the students can see, touch and compare. **STEAM:** Provide the students with 3-5 beans (Kidney or Lima), let them soak the beans in some water, then ask them to wet a paper towel and place the bean inside the wet paper towel. Now place the paper towel and bean inside a Ziplock bag. Tape the Ziplock bag to the wall or a window (at child's eye level) and let the students know that you will observe the plant daily and measure its growth on a growth chart. Finally, ask the students to draw a picture of what they think their bean plant will look like when it grows up. Place the drawings next to the bag.	Beans (you may want to soak overnight depending on the type of bean) , Ziplock bags, paper towel, paper, crayons	Assessment Photo

STANDARDS	TIME	CIRCLE TIME ACTIVITIES	MATERIALS	DOCUMENTATION
Cognitive Development Language Development Gross Motor Development Social/Emotional Dev.		**CIRCLE TIME:** **1.** Calendar Activities(Days, Months, Counting, Number Recognition, Patterns, Season, Year) -Spin around while counting the days in the month -Incorporate exercise and counting by 10's such as count by 10's while touching their toes. **2.** Music & Movement Recommended:	Calendar, colored calendar numbers, music source	Assessment Photo
Cognitive Development Language Development Social/Emotional Dev.		**Story Time:** Books about plants, seeds, farms, growing, etc.		Assessment Photo

STANDARDS	TIME	EXTRA ACTIVITIES	MATERIALS	DOCUMENTATION

Name Recognition and Practice

_____

Number Recognition and Practice

6_____ **7**_____ **8**_____

9_____ **10**_____

Letter Review and Practice

M_____ **N**_____

O_____

31. Relevant Writing 2

Can you think of something black?

_____ is black.

Sight word recognition and practice.

Black_____

*Encourage student to draw a picture of something black on the next page.

31. Week 31 Shopping List

ITEMS	YES, we have this item	NO, we need to buy	$ COST Of item	ITEMS	YES, we have this item	NO, we need to buy	$ COST Of item
PROVOCATION: Homemade playdough fresh herbs				SENSORY: Water watercolor rose petals cut oranges blades of grass wooden spoons			
MORNING MEETING: Music device White-board chart paper sharpie dry-erase marker				PROCESS ART: Cut vegetables paint plates construction paper			
WRITING: Highlighter chart paper Pencils				STEAM: Beans Ziplock bags paper towel paper crayons			

31. Parent Letter

Dear Family,

This week we will be talking about growing vegetables. We will explore the question, "What do our vegetables need to grow?" Students will plant their own beans in a bag and monitor the growth. This is a great week for you to visit a farmer's market with your child and talk about the vegetables you see and where they come from.

Provocation: Herbal Playdough!	Sensory: Nature Fairy Soup!	Letter/Word Focus: Review M, N, O / Black
Process Art: Vegetable Printmaking!	STEM Project: Plant Beans!	Writing: _____ is black.

DAILY SCHEDULE & PLANS

STANDARDS	TIME	DAILY ACTIVITIES	MATERIALS	DOCUMENTATION
Cognitive Development Language Development Fine Motor Development	------	**Weekly Transition:** Continue sight word recognition. Write the sight words on an index card. Only Choose 3-5 for the week to practice. Ask the student to identify the sight word before transitioning. *You may also use this time to continue to review letter recognition and letter depending on where your students are.	Index cards, sharpie	Assessment
Cognitive Development Sensory Development	------	**Extension Center:** *What was successful and interesting to students last week? Carry this over to a center this week, so the students may extend this play/learning.*		Assessment Photo
Cognitive Development Language Development Gross Motor Development Sensory Development Social/Emotional Dev. Fine Motor Development		**Provocation:** Down on the Farm! Place some playdough (brown, green, and blue) in bowls along with a few sticks, stones, craft sticks for possible fencing and several farm animals. Invite students to create their own farm. This can be done as a group or you may place a piece of cardboard or cardstock at each student's seat for independent creations.	Playdough (green, brown, blue), sticks, stones, craft sticks, farm animals	Assessment Photo
Cognitive Development Language Development Sensory Development Fine Motor Development		**Morning Meeting:** 1. Good morning song (Teacher's choice) 2. Monday: Morning Message **Letter/Word Focus:** Review P, Q, R; Pink 3. Tues-Fri: **"My News"** /Writing Prompt: _____ is pink.	Music device, white-board, chart paper, sharpie, dry-erase marker	Assessment Photo

STANDARDS	TIME	OUTDOOR ACTIVITIES	MATERIALS	DOCUMENTATION
Cognitive Development Language Development Sensory Development Fine Motor Development		Outdoor time/Free Choice: *Optional activities include: watering plants, pulling weeds, gardening, sensory, snow painting, snowman building, snow shoveling, raking leaves, etc.* **Extra Activities:**		Assessment Photo

STANDARDS	TIME	LEARNING CENTER ACTIVITY CHOICES	MATERIALS	DOCUMENTATION
Cognitive Development Language Development Fine Motor Development		**WRITING:** Name, Letter Focus, My News/Writing Prompt. Use relevant writing sheets to complete writing time or allow the students time to freely draw and the teacher to dictate the students' drawing. Teacher can use the dictation to encourage identification of letters and words along with independent writing. **MATH:** Also, use the Math sheet. This should be used along with dice. Give the student one die and ask him/her to roll it, set it above the first box and have the student write the number of dots in the box. Give the student a second die and ask him/her to repeat the same process for the second box. Then ask the student to slide the 2 dice down the sheet and over the 3rd box (after the equals sign) and ask them to count all the dots together and write the number. Continue this process until	Highlighter, chart paper from **My News,** pencils Dice	Assessment Photo

262

	all the addition problems are completed.		
Cognitive Development Sensory Development	**SENSORY:** Milk the Cow! Place the sensory bin on the floor and place a chair at each end. Place a pole on top of the chairs to create a bridge across the sensory bin (You may want to secure the pole with duct tape to keep from rolling). Now fill a couple latex gloves with water. Tie the wrist of the gloves in a knot to hold the water in and using string or duct tape secure the gloves (udders) onto the pole, so they appear to be cow utters. Now use a pin to poke a hole in the end of each finger. Let the milking begin! Let the students explore milking the udders into the sensory bin.	Pole, 2 chairs, duct tape, string, latex gloves	Assessment Photo
Cognitive Development Language Development Gross Motor Development Sensory Development Social/Emotional Dev. Fine Motor Development	**Learning Centers:** *Note any changes and/or additions made to learning centers*		Assessment Photo
Cognitive Development Language Development Sensory Development Fine Motor Development	**PROCESS ART:** Cow Inspired Art! Provide the students with black construction paper pieces (cut into 4ths), scissors, glue with paint brush for application, , paper plates, black and pink markers and some googly eyes to create their own cow or black & white art.	Paper plates, black construction paper, scissors, black & pink markers, googly eyes, glue, paint brush	Assessment Photo
Cognitive Development Language Development Sensory Development Social/Emotional Dev. Fine Motor Development	**Question:** Where does milk come from? How do we get butter? **View:** Use the internet to view cows being milked and butter being made. **STEAM:** Let's Make Butter! Provide the students with	Mason/jelly jars with lids, heavy whipping cream, crackers, spoons	Assessment Photo

small jelly or mason jars. Help them to pour the whipping cream into the jars (½ full) and place the lid tightly on. Now provide several different ways for the students to shake the jars. They can sit on the floor and roll the jars to each other. They can carefully shake the jars, jump with the jars. The students will want to shake the jars until they no longer hear the liquid moving and there is butter! When the butter is ready you may pour off any excess liquid and then provide the students crackers and a spoon to taste their butter.

STANDARDS	TIME	CIRCLE TIME ACTIVITIES	MATERIALS	DOCUMENTATION
Cognitive Development Language Development Gross Motor Development Social/Emotional Dev.		**CIRCLE TIME:** 1. Calendar Activities (Days, Months, Counting, Number Recognition, Patterns, Season, Year)	Calendar, colored calendar numbers, music source	Assessment Photo
		-Do knee lifts while counting the days in the month		
		-Incorporate exercise and counting by 10's such as count by 10's while doing sit-ups.		
		2. Music & Movement Recommended:		
Cognitive Development Language Development Social/Emotional Dev.		**Story Time:** Books farms, farm animals, cows, barns, etc.		Assessment Photo

32. Relevant Writing 1

Name Recognition and Practice

_____

Letter Review and Practice

P_____

Q_____

R_____

32. Relevant Writing 2

Can you think of something pink?

_____ is pink.

Sight word recognition and practice.

Pink

_____

*Encourage student to draw a picture of something pink on the next page.

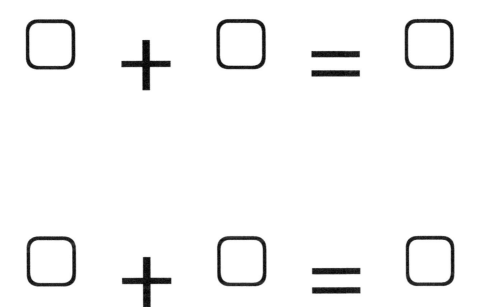

32. Week 32 Shopping List

ITEMS	YES, we have this item	NO, we need to buy	$ COST Of item	ITEMS	YES, we have this item	NO, we need to buy	$ COST Of item
PROVOCATION: Playdough (green, brown, blue), sticks, stones, craft sticks, farm animals				SENSORY: Pole, 2 chairs, duct tape, string, latex gloves			
MORNING MEETING: Music device White-board chart paper sharpie dry-erase marker				PROCESS ART: Paper plates, black construction paper, scissors, black & pink markers, googly eyes, glue, paint brush			
WRITING: Highlighter chart paper Pencils dice				STEAM: Mason/jelly jars with lids, heavy whipping cream, crackers, spoons			

32. Parent Letter

Dear Family,

This week we will be talking about farm animals, especially cows. We will explore the question, "Where does our milk come from?" Students will learn to milk a cow and make their own butter! This is a great week to visit a local farm with your child.

Provocation: Down on the Farm!	**Sensory:** Milk the Cow!	**Letter/Word Focus:** Review P, Q, R / Pink
Process Art: Cow Inspired Art	**STEM Project:** Let's Make Butter!	**Writing:** _____ is pink.

DAILY SCHEDULE & PLANS

STANDARDS	TIME	DAILY ACTIVITIES	MATERIALS	DOCUMENTATION
Cognitive Development Language Development Fine Motor Development	------	**Weekly Transition:** Number recognition. Write numbers 1-30 on an index card. Only Choose 3-5 for the week to practice. Ask the student to identify the number before transitioning. *You may also use this time to choose 2 numbers for students to add together depending on where the students are.*	Index cards, sharpie	Assessment
Cognitive Development Sensory Development	------	**Extension Center:** *What was successful and interesting to students last week? Carry this over to a center this week, so the students may extend this play/learning.*		Assessment Photo
Cognitive Development Language Development Gross Motor Development Sensory Development Social/Emotional Dev. Fine Motor Development		**Provocation:** Name recognition. Write each student's name on an index card and place in a basket on the table. Using a Sharpie write corresponding letters on rocks to place in a bowl and let the student match each rock letter to the letter on the index card to spell their friends' names. Provide additional index cards and pencil/marker for the student to write their name themselves. Encourage students to match and write their friends' names and/or sight words.	Rocks, index cards, Sharpies, bowls/baskets, pencils/markers	Assessment Photo
Cognitive Development Language Development Sensory Development Fine Motor Development		**Morning Meeting:** 1. Good morning song (Teacher's choice) 2. Monday: Morning Message **Letter/Word Focus:** Review S, T, U; Orange 3. Tues-Fri: **"My News"** **/Writing Prompt:** _____ is orange.	Music device, white-board, chart paper, sharpie, dry-erase marker	Assessment Photo

272

STANDARDS	TIME	OUTDOOR ACTIVITIES	MATERIALS	DOCUMENTATION
Cognitive Development Language Development Sensory Development Fine Motor Development		Outdoor time/Free Choice:		Assessment Photo
		Optional activities include: watering plants, pulling weeds, gardening, sensory, snow painting, snowman building, snow shoveling, raking leaves, etc. **Extra Activities:**		

STANDARDS	TIME	LEARNING CENTER ACTIVITY CHOICES	MATERIALS	DOCUMENTATION
Cognitive Development Language Development Fine Motor Development		**WRITING:** Name, Letter Focus, My News/Writing Prompt. Use relevant writing sheets to complete writing time or allow the students time to freely draw and the teacher to dictate the students' drawing. Teacher can use the dictation to encourage identification of letters and words along with independent writing.	Highlighter, chart paper from **My News,** pencils	Assessment Photo
Cognitive Development Language Development Fine Motor Development		**NUMBERS/MATH:** Use math sheets to add numbers. This should be used along with dice. Give the student one die and ask him/her to roll it, set it above the first box and have the student write the number of dots in the box. Give the student a second die and ask him/her to repeat the same process for the second box. Then ask the student to slide the 2 dice down the sheet and over the 3rd box (after the equals sign) and ask them to count all the dots together and write the number. Continue this process until all the addition problems are completed.	Dice	Assessment Photo

273

Cognitive Development Sensory Development	SENSORY: Raining snakes and frogs! Fill the bottom of the sensory tub with water. Add a few leaves, pretend frogs & snakes. Last provide a couple plastic/foam cups with holes poked in the bottom. Children can fill the cups with water and let the water drip out of the holes to simulate rain.	Pretend frogs & snakes, water, plastic/foam cups	Assessment Photo
Cognitive Development Language Development Gross Motor Development Sensory Development Social/Emotional Dev. Fine Motor Development	Learning Centers: *Note any changes and/or additions made to learning centers*		Assessment Photo
Cognitive Development Language Development Sensory Development Fine Motor Development	PROCESS ART: Q-tip snake paint. Using construction paper/cardstock/paper plate cut out a snake pattern or let the student draw their own snake. Provide students with a variety of paint colors and Q-tips for application. Demonstrate dipping the Q-tip in the paint and then dotting the paint onto the snake pattern. Students may dot their snake or may use the Q-tip like a paintbrush.	Paint, Q-tips, construction paper/cardstock/ paper plate, scissors	Assessment Photo
Cognitive Development Language Development Sensory Development Social/Emotional Dev. Fine Motor Development	Question of the Day: Why does it rain? View: Use the internet to view water cycle, again. STEAM: Terrarium in a jar! Have each student bring a small jar with a lid. Provide the students with pebbles,	Herb seeds, small jars with lids, soil, pebbles, sand, water	Assessment Photo

sand and soil. Let the students layer their jars with pebbles and sand then topsoil. Provide the students with herb seeds such as basil, rosemary, thyme or your favorite. Let them sprinkle the seeds on top of the soil and mist or sprinkle with water. Close the lid tight and keep in the classroom for a couple of weeks to show how the water moves to the top of the jar and fall back to the soil just like the water cycle. Once the herbs have grown open the jars and have a taste test.

STANDARDS	TIME	CIRCLE TIME ACTIVITIES	MATERIALS	DOCUMENTATION
Cognitive Development Language Development Gross Motor Development Social/Emotional Dev.		**CIRCLE TIME:** **1.** Calendar Activities (Days, Months, Counting, Number Recognition, Patterns, Season, Year) -Have students tap their head while counting the days in the month -Incorporate exercise and counting by 10's such as count by 10's while hopping like a frog.	Calendar, colored calendar numbers, music source	Assessment Photo
Cognitive Development Language Development Social/Emotional Dev.		**2.** Music & Movement: **Story Time:** Books about snakes, monkeys, rainforests, tree frogs, etc.		Assessment Photo

STANDARDS	TIME	EXTRA ACTIVITIES	MATERIALS	DOCUMENTATION

275

33. Relevant Writing 1

Name Recognition and Practice

_____

Letter Review and Practice

S_____

T_____

U_____

33. Relevant Writing 2

Can you think of something orange?

_____is orange.

Sight word recognition and practice.

Orange _____

*Encourage student to draw a picture of something pink on the next page.

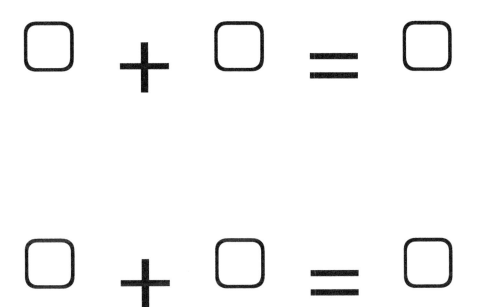

33. Week 33 Shopping List

ITEMS	YES, we have this item	NO, we need to buy	$ COST Of item	ITEMS	YES, we have this item	NO, we need to buy	$ COST Of item
PROVOCATION: Rocks index cards Sharpies bowls/baskets pencils/markers				SENSORY: Pretend frogs & snakes Water plastic/foam cups			
MORNING MEETING: Music device White-board chart paper sharpie dry-erase marker				PROCESS ART: Paint, Q-tips construction paper/cardstock/ paper plate scissors			
WRITING: Highlighter chart paper Pencils dice				STEAM: Herb seeds small jars with lids soil Pebbles Sand water			

33. Parent Letter

Dear Family,

This week we will be talking about the rainforest! You can discuss the animals that live in the rainforest such as snakes, frogs, birds, butterflies, etc. You may even want to follow up the topic with a trip to the zoo!

Provocation: Recognizing & writing friends' names	Sensory: Raining snakes and frogs!	Letter/Word Focus: Review S, T, U / Orange
Process Art: Snake Art	STEM Project: Making a terrarium	Writing: _____ is orange.

DAILY SCHEDULE & PLANS

STANDARDS	TIME	DAILY ACTIVITIES	MATERIALS	DOCUMENTATION
Cognitive Development Language Development Fine Motor Development	------	**Weekly Transition:** Letter, word & number recognition. Alternate your letter cards, sight word cards, and numbers 1-30 cards when asking students to transition. Have them identify the letter, word or number on the card.	Letter, word, & number cards	
Cognitive Development Sensory Development	------	**Extension Center:**		
		What was successful and interesting to students last week? Carry this over to a center this week, so the students may extend this play/learning.		
Cognitive Development Language Development Gross Motor Development Sensory Development Social/Emotional Dev. Fine Motor Development		**Provocation:** Replicate a famous artist. Choose a famous painting and print in full color to place on the table. Provide only the paint colors found in the painting. Place each paint in a separate jar with a separate paintbrush. Ask the students to paint what they see.	Color printed image of a famous painting, paint colors, paintbrushes, construction paper	
Cognitive Development Language Development Sensory Development Fine Motor Development		**Morning Meeting:** 1. Good morning song (Teacher's choice) 2. Monday: Morning Message **Letter/Word Focus:** Review V, W, X; Purple 3. Tues-Fri: **"My News"** **/Writing Prompt:** _____ is purple.	Music device, white-board, chart paper, sharpie, dry-erase marker	

282

STANDARDS	TIME	OUTDOOR ACTIVITIES	MATERIALS	DOCUMENTATION
Cognitive Development Language Development Sensory Development Fine Motor Development		Outdoor time/Free Choice: *Optional activities include: watering plants, pulling weeds, gardening, sensory, snow painting, snowman building, snow shoveling, raking leaves, etc. **Extra Activities:**		

STANDARDS	TIME	LEARNING CENTER ACTIVITY CHOICES	MATERIALS	DOCUMENTATION
Cognitive Development Language Development Fine Motor Development		**WRITING:** Name, Letter Focus, My News/Writing Prompt. Use relevant writing sheets to complete writing time or allow the students time to freely draw and the teacher to dictate the students' drawing. Teacher can use the dictation to encourage identification of letters and words along with independent writing.	Highlighter, chart paper from **My News,** pencils	
Cognitive Development Language Development Fine Motor Development		**NUMBERS/MATH:** Use math sheets to subtract numbers. You will need beans or counters for this activity. Write numbers in the boxes on the math sheet (the numbers will depend upon the level of the student you are working with). Ask the student to count out the number of beans in the first box. Then teach the student the subtraction sign means to take away. Have the student identify the number in the second box and remove that number of beans from the	Beans or counters	

pile. Last, have the student count the remainder of the beans and write the final number in the last box after the equal sign.

Cognitive Development Sensory Development	**SENSORY:** Pond Life. Place river rock, water, plastic frogs & fish, and small nets in the sensory bin. You can tint the water green by adding green watercolor or food coloring. The children can use the river rocks to build in the pond. This is a great time to for open discussion about what you might find in a pond or how fish breathe in water.	River rocks, plastic frogs & fish, small nets, green watercolor or food coloring
Cognitive Development Language Development Gross Motor Development Sensory Development Social/Emotional Dev. Fine Motor Development	**Learning Centers:** *Note any changes and/or additions made to learning centers*	
Cognitive Development Language Development Sensory Development Fine Motor Development	**PROCESS ART:** Gift for Mom or a special female. Pressed flowers. Provide students with a variety of flowers, petals, blades of grass, and leaves from plants. Cut a 16" X 11" piece of clear contact paper. Use a Sharpie to draw a line down the middle of the paper. Instruct students to arrange the petals, flowers, etc. onto the sticky side of the contact paper. You can use the line drawn down the middle to instruct them to only place the flowers onto one section	Flower petals, blades of grass, and leaves from plants, Clear contact paper, Duct tape (black, white or colorful)

Cognitive Development
Language Development
Sensory Development
Social/Emotional Dev.
Fine Motor Development

of the paper, so you can easily fold it over to preserve the artwork. Once they are finished fold the contact paper along the drawn line. You can create a framed edge by using black, white or colorful Duct tape. This can be a gift for the student to give that special female in his/her life.

Question of the Day: What do you find in a river? Make a list on the board or chart paper

Heavy plastic or aluminum foil, big and small rocks, bag of sand, sticks, water source (hydrant & hose)

View: Use the internet to view a flowing river, stream or creek.

STEAM: Build a river. This activity is best completed outdoors with a water source. If you have no outdoor space then you could use s plastic baby pool to contain the project. You will need enough aluminum foil or heavy plastic to roll out about 8'-12'. This project can be created in a sand area, rock area or grass. Simply have the students help you roll out the plastic/aluminum foil. Haves students use the river rocks, sand and sticks to build up the sides. Place the water source at one end of the plastic and turn the water source (hydrant & hose) on very low, so the students can observe where the water is flowing. Let them use their imagination to build in and around the water flow. They will be amazed at their power to change the flow of water with rocks, sticks, and sand.

STANDARDS	TIME	CIRCLE TIME ACTIVITIES	MATERIALS	DOCUMENTATION
Cognitive Development Language Development Gross Motor Development Social/Emotional Dev.		**CIRCLE TIME:** **1.** Calendar Activities (Days, Months, Counting, Number Recognition, Patterns, Season, Year) -Have students touch their elbows to their knees while counting the days in the month. -Incorporate exercise and counting by 10's such as count by 10's while	Calendar, colored calendar numbers, music source	
Cognitive Development Language Development Social/Emotional Dev.		**2.** Music & Movement: **Story Time:** Books about rivers, ponds, fish , frogs, mom, grandma, family		

STANDARDS	TIME	EXTRA ACTIVITIES	MATERIALS	DOCUMENTATION

34. Relevant Writing 1

Name Recognition and Practice

_____

Letter Review and Practice

V _____

W _____

X _____

34. Relevant Writing 2

Can you think of something purple?

_____is purple.

Sight word recognition and practice.

Purple _____

*Encourage student to draw a picture of something purple on the next page.

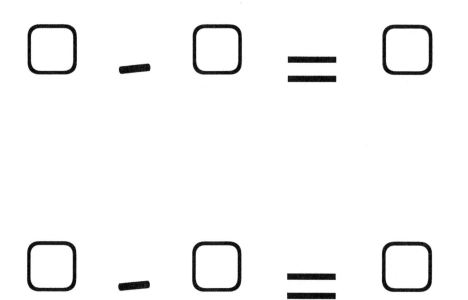

34. Week 34 Shopping List

ITEMS	YES, we have this item	NO, we need to buy	$ COST Of item	ITEMS	YES, we have this item	NO, we need to buy	$ COST Of item
PROVOCATION: Color printed image of a famous painting paint colors paintbrushes construction paper				SENSORY: River rocks plastic frogs & fish small nets			
				green watercolor or food coloring			
MORNING MEETING: Music device White-board chart paper sharpie dry-erase marker				PROCESS ART: Flower petals, blades of grass, and leaves from plants			
WRITING: Highlighter chart paper Pencils beans/counters				Clear contact paper Duct tape (black, white or colorful)			
				STEAM: Heavy plastic or aluminum foil			
				big & small rocks bag of sand Sticks water source (hydrant & hose)			

34. Parent Letter

Dear Family,

This week your child will build a river! We will talk about what we find in a river and discover how the water flows in a river, creek or stream. This would be a great time for you and your child to observe and explore a creek, river or stream. What happens if you place a big rock in the middle of the stream?

Provocation: Let's replicate a famous painting!	**Sensory:** Playing in the pond!	**Letter/Word Focus:** Review V, W, X / Purple
Process Art: A gift for a special female in my life.	**STEM Project:** Build a river!	**Writing:** _____ is purple.

DAILY SCHEDULE & PLANS

STANDARDS	TIME	DAILY ACTIVITIES	MATERIALS	DOCUMENTATION
Cognitive Development Language Development Fine Motor Development	------	**Weekly Transition:** Rhyming. Pick a word such as "cat" and have each child give you a word that rhymes with "cat". Silly words count, too!		
Cognitive Development Sensory Development	------	**Extension Center:** *What was successful and interesting to students last week? Carry this over to a center this week, so the students may extend this play/learning.*		
Cognitive Development Language Development Gross Motor Development Sensory Development Social/Emotional Dev. Fine Motor Development		**Provocation:** The Branch. Place a large branch on the table. Provide the students with bright, colorful paints in jars and paintbrushes. Encourage students to paint the branch, so it can be hung in the classroom. This can be a great gift to the school from the class of ____.	Large branch, jars of paint, paintbrushes	
Cognitive Development Language Development Sensory Development Fine Motor Development		**Morning Meeting:** 1. Good morning song (Teacher's choice) 2. Monday: Morning Message **Letter/Word Focus:** Review Y,Z; white 3. Tues-Fri: **"My News"** /Writing Prompt: _____ is white.	Music device, white-board, chart paper, sharpie, dry-erase marker	

STANDARDS	TIME	OUTDOOR ACTIVITIES	MATERIALS	DOCUMENTATION
Cognitive Development Language Development Sensory Development Fine Motor Development		Outdoor time/Free Choice:		

293

Optional activities include: watering plants, pulling weeds, gardening, sensory, snow painting, snowman building, snow shoveling, raking leaves, etc.

Extra Activities:

STANDARDS	TIME	LEARNING CENTER ACTIVITY CHOICES	MATERIALS	DOCUMENTATION
Cognitive Development Language Development Fine Motor Development		**WRITING:** Name, Letter Focus, My News/Writing Prompt. Use relevant writing sheets to complete writing time or allow the students time to freely draw and the teacher to dictate the students' drawing. Teacher can use the dictation to encourage identification of letters and words along with independent writing.	Highlighter, chart paper from **My News,** pencils	
Cognitive Development Language Development Fine Motor Development		**NUMBERS/MATH:** Use math sheets to subtract numbers. You will need beans or counters for this activity. Write numbers in the boxes on the math sheet (the numbers will depend upon the level of the student you are working with). Ask the student to count out the number of beans in the first box. Then teach the student the subtraction sign means to take away. Have the student identify the number in the second box and remove that number of beans from the pile. Last, have the student count the remainder of the beans and write the final number in the last box after the equal sign.	Beans or counters	
Cognitive Development Sensory Development		**SENSORY:** The ocean. Place sand, shells, plastic sea turtles, small umbrellas (drink umbrellas without a point on the end), measuring cups, funnels, and small shovels. This a great time for open discussions about the	Sand, shells, plastic sea turtles, drink umbrellas (w/out a pointed end), measuring cups, funnels, small shovels	

294

ocean. Who has visited the
ocean? What creatures live in
the ocean?

Cognitive Development
Language Development
Gross Motor Development
Sensory Development
Social/Emotional Dev.
Fine Motor Development

Learning Centers:
*Note any changes and/or
additions made to learning
centers*

Cognitive Development
Language Development
Sensory Development
Fine Motor Development

PROCESS ART: Sand
paint. Provide the student
with a blue piece of
construction paper or
cardstock, glue,
paintbrushes, and a tray to
work on. Have the students
dip the paintbrush into the
glue and paint a picture onto
the blue paper. Then give
them sand to sprinkle onto
their paper. When they finish
raise the paper up and let the
sand fall onto the tray
revealing their sand art.

Blue construction
paper/cardstock, sand, glue,
paintbrushes, tray

Cognitive Development
Language Development
Sensory Development
Social/Emotional Dev.
Fine Motor Development

Question of the Day: Show
the students vegetable oil.
Using a spoon put a drop on
in their finger. Ask them
how it feels? Then ask them
to wash it off with water and
no soap. Was it easy?

Bins/containers, water
vegetable oil, feathers, spoon,
soap, washcloths

295

View: Use the internet to view an oil spill in the ocean.

STEAM: Oil spill. Use one large container or a small container for each student. Fill the container 1/3rd full of water. Poor enough vegetable oil into the container to cover the surface. Give the students a spoon and see if they can scoop out the oil. Now provide the students with some feathers to symbolize birds and ask them to dunk the feathers into the oil spill. Now ask them to try and clean the feathers. Provide a washcloth, soap, and water in a clean water bin. Discuss the outcome of the project.

STANDARDS	TIME	CIRCLE TIME ACTIVITIES	MATERIALS	DOCUMENTATION
Cognitive Development **Language Development** **Gross Motor Development** **Social/Emotional Dev.**		**CIRCLE TIME:** 1. Calendar Activities (Days, Months, Counting, Number Recognition, Patterns, Season, Year)	Calendar, colored calendar numbers, music source	
		-Have students do jumping jacks while counting the days in the month		
		-Incorporate exercise and counting by 10's such as count by 10's while		
		2. Music & Movement:		
Cognitive Development **Language Development** **Social/Emotional Dev.**		**Story Time:** Books about ocean, ocean creatures, sand, oil spills, shells, vacations		

35. Relevant Writing 1

Name Recognition and Practice

_____

Letter Review and Practice

Y_____

Z_____

35. Relevant Writing 2

Can you think of something white?

_____is white.

Sight word recognition and practice.

white _____

*Encourage student to draw a picture of something white on the next page.

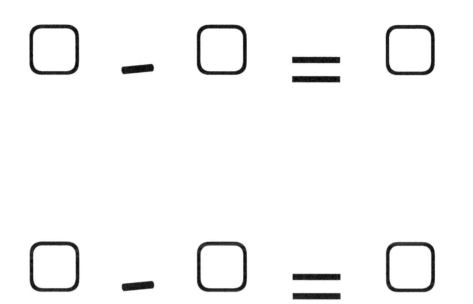

35. Week 35 Shopping List

ITEMS	YES, we have this item	NO, we need to buy	$ COST Of item	ITEMS	YES, we have this item	NO, we need to buy	$ COST Of item
PROVOCATION: Large branch jars of paint paintbrushes				**SENSORY:** Sand Shells plastic sea turtles drink umbrellas (w/out a pointed end) measuring cups funnels small shovels			
MORNING MEETING: Music device White-board chart paper sharpie dry-erase marker				**PROCESS ART:** Blue construction paper/cardstock			
WRITING: Highlighter chart paper Pencils beans/counters				Sand Glue Paintbrushes trays **STEAM:** Bins/containers water vegetable oil feathers Spoon Soap washcloths			

35. Parent Letter

Dear Family,

This week you child will explore the ocean! They will create sand paintings and discover what an oil spill is. This is a great time to discuss a previous or future trip to the ocean. You can use the internet to show your child videos and pictures of the ocean. Show them different locations such as East Coast beaches, West Coach beaches, and the Caribbean.

Provocation: The Branch!	Sensory: The Ocean!	Letter/Word Focus: Review Y, Z / White
Process Art: Sand Painting.	STEM Project: Oil Spill!	Writing: _____ is purple.

DAILY SCHEDULE & PLANS

STANDARDS	TIME	DAILY ACTIVITIES	MATERIALS	DOCUMENTATION
Cognitive Development Language Development Fine Motor Development	------	**Weekly Transition:** Birth month. Ask the students, "If you were born in the month of _____ then you may………. (line up, wash your hands, etc.,)"	list of birthdays	
Cognitive Development Sensory Development	------	**Extension Center:**		
		What was successful and interesting to students last week? Carry this over to a center this week, so the students may extend this play/learning.		
Cognitive Development Language Development Gross Motor Development Sensory Development Social/Emotional Dev. Fine Motor Development		**Provocation:** Ocean dough. Provide blue playdough and bowls or divided tray of shells, sand, sand dollars, starfish, sea creatures, blue & clear glass beads, etc. These items can be plastic or real. Let the children create their own ocean scenes.	Blue playdough, divided tray, sand, sand dollars, starfish, sea creatures, blue/clear glass beads	
Cognitive Development Language Development Sensory Development Fine Motor Development		**Morning Meeting:** 1. Good morning song (Teacher's choice) 2. Monday: Morning Message **Letter/Word Focus:** Review sight words 3. Tues-Fri: **"My News"** /**Writing Prompt:** What do you like most about school?	Music device, white-board, chart paper, sharpie, dry-erase marker	

STANDARDS	TIME	OUTDOOR ACTIVITIES	MATERIALS	DOCUMENTATION
Cognitive Development Language Development Sensory Development Fine Motor Development		Outdoor time/Free Choice: *Optional activities include: watering plants, pulling weeds, gardening, sensory, snow painting, snowman building, snow shoveling, raking leaves, etc.* **Extra Activities:**		

STANDARDS	TIME	LEARNING CENTER ACTIVITY CHOICES	MATERIALS	DOCUMENTATION
Cognitive Development Language Development Fine Motor Development		**WRITING:** Name, Letter Focus, My News/Writing Prompt. Use relevant writing sheets to complete writing time or allow the students time to freely draw and the teacher to dictate the students' drawing. Teacher can use the dictation to encourage identification of letters and words along with independent writing.	Highlighter, chart paper from **My News,** pencils	
Cognitive Development Language Development Fine Motor Development		**NUMBERS/MATH:** Use math sheets to subtract numbers. You will need beans or counters for this activity. Write numbers in the boxes on the math sheet (the numbers will depend upon the level of the student you are working with). Ask the student to count out the number of beans in the first box. Then teach the student the subtraction sign means to take away. Have the student identify the number in the second box and remove that number of beans from the	Beans or counters	

305

pile. Last, have the student count the remainder of the beans and write the final number in the last box after the equal sign.

Cognitive Development Sensory Development	**SENSORY:** Under water. Fill the sensory bin half full of blue water beads. Hide plastic ocean animals, shells with letters printed on them under the beads. Add a couple of boats to the top along with some spoons and measuring cups. Encourage sensory play and questions about the animals found in the ocean along with a search for letters!	Blue water beads, plastic ocean animals, shells w/ letters printed on them
Cognitive Development Language Development Gross Motor Development Sensory Development Social/Emotional Dev. Fine Motor Development	**Learning Centers:** *Note any changes and/or additions made to learning centers*	
Cognitive Development Language Development Sensory Development Fine Motor Development	**PROCESS ART:** A gift for a special male in my life. Portraits. Have students bring a picture of their father, grandfather or a special male in their life. Have the students look at the pictures and answer questions about	Cardstock, pencils, Fine point Sharpies

Cognitive Development
Language Development
Sensory Development
Social/Emotional Dev.
Fine Motor Development

eye color, hair color, etc. Then provide the students pencils to draw a portrait of their special male friend. Last, provide the students with fine point Sharpies to trace their pencil drawing. You can also add "I love my Dad (grandpa, uncle) because_____."

Question of the Day: What is a tower? How tall should the tower be?

View: Use the internet to view towers such as the Eiffel Tower and the Leaning Tower of Pisa

STEAM: Provide the students with 20-50 plastic or Styrofoam cups, cardstock cut into different size squares. This activity can be done in groups or individually. Demonstrate by setting 4 cups on the floor in a square shape, laying the cardstock on top of the cups, then placing 3 cups on top of the cardstock in a triangular shape, placing another piece of cardstock on top of the 3 cups, then 2 more cups, and so on until you create a pyramid shape. Let students explore different ways to build towers with the cups and cards stock. Who's tower is the tallest?

100 plastic/Styrofoam cups (this # may vary depending on the # of students), cardstock cut into different size squares

STANDARDS	TIME	CIRCLE TIME ACTIVITIES	MATERIALS	DOCUMENTATION
Cognitive Development Language Development Gross Motor Development Social/Emotional Dev.		**CIRCLE TIME:** **1.** Calendar Activities (Days, Months, Counting, Number Recognition, Patterns, Season, Year) -Have students hop on one foot while counting the days of the month -Incorporate exercise and counting by 10's such as count by 10's while **2.** Music & Movement:	Calendar, colored calendar numbers, music source	
Cognitive Development Language Development Social/Emotional Dev.		**Story Time:** Books about ocean, ocean creatures, scuba diving, father's, grandfathers, towers, construction.		

STANDARDS	TIME	EXTRA ACTIVITIES	MATERIALS	DOCUMENTATION

36. Relevant Writing 1

Name Recognition and Practice

_____

Write your letters. Writing can continue on the back of this page.

36. Relevant Writing 2

What do you like most about school?

I like_____.

*Encourage student to draw what they like about school on the next page.

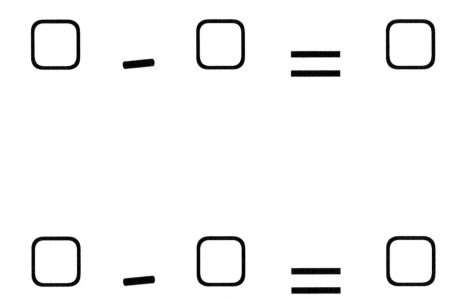

36. Week 36 Shopping List

ITEMS	YES, we have this item	NO, we need to buy	$ COST Of item	ITEMS	YES, we have this item	NO, we need to buy	$ COST Of item
PROVOCATION: Blue playdough divided tray Sand sand dollars Starfish sea creatures blue/clear glass beads				SENSORY: Blue water beads plastic ocean animals			
				shells w/ letters printed on them			
MORNING MEETING: Music device White-board chart paper sharpie dry-erase marker				PROCESS ART: Cardstock Pencils			
				Fine point Sharpies			
WRITING: Highlighter chart paper Pencils beans/counters				STEAM: 100 plastic/Styrofoam cups (this # may vary depending on the # of students)			
				cardstock cut into different size squares			

36. Parent Letter

Dear Family,

This week your child will explore the creatures of the ocean along with building a tower! How tall do you think our tower will be? This is a great time to take a walk around your city or town and compare the size of the buildings. You may even spot some construction going on!

Provocation: Ocean dough!	Sensory: Under water!	Letter/Word Focus: Write your letters
Process Art: A gift for that special male in my life.	STEM Project: Build a Tower!	Writing: What do you like most about school?

Assessment Tool

Children develop and acquire different skills at different ages. This assessment tool should be used as a tracker, but should not be used to exclusively determine a child's development. This is a compiled list of items to help the teacher track development and skills. Some teachers/parents choose to use a tool to better understand the development of a child while others may choose to use a portfolio or other tool to determine development and acquired skills.

	Date of Assessment	Assessor	Child's Age (Years, months)
1			
2			
3			
4			
5			
6			
7			

Transpiring = *Student attempts the skill*

Progressing = *Student can partially complete the skill or can complete the skill with help*

Accomplished = *Student can complete the skill with no help*

Skills (Ages 3-5)

Skill	Transpiring	Progressing	Accomplished
Name Recognition			
Holding Pencil			
Writing Name			
Using Scissors			
Table Manners			
Setting Table			

Rhyming			
Adding			
Subtracting			
Count to 30			

Number Recognition Ages 3-5)

1	2	3	4	5	6	7	8	9	10

Colors (Ages 3-5)

Red	Yellow	Blue	Green	white	black	purple	orange	pink

Shapes (Ages 3-5)

Circle	Square	Triangle	Rectangle	Oval	Star	Diamond

Letter Recognition (Ages 3-5) & Phonics (Ages 4-5)

Place the uppercase and lowercase letter under the appropriate section (Transpiring, Progressing, Accomplished. EXAMPLE:

Letter	Transpiring	Progressing	Accomplished
D,d-Recognition	d		D

Letter	Transpiring	Progressing	Accomplished
D,d-Recognition			
D-Phonics			
O,o-Recognition			
O-Phonics			
C,c- Recognition			

316

Letter	Transpiring	Progressing	Accomplished
C- Phonics			
G,g-Recognition			
G-Phonics			
A,a-Recognition			
A-Phonics			
T,t-Recognition			
T-Phonics			
M,m- Recognition			
M- Phonics			
L,l- Recognition			
L- Phonics			
U,u- Recognition			
U- Phonics			
E,e- Recognition			
E- Phonics			
I,i- Recognition			
I- Phonics			
Rr- Recognition			
R- Phonics			
F,f- Recognition			
F- Phonics			
B,b- Recognition			

Letter	Transpiring	Progressing	Accomplished
B- Phonics			
N,n- Recognition			
N- Phonics			
H,h- Recognition			
H- Phonics			
Letter	Transpiring	Progressing	Accomplished
V,v- Recognition			
V- Phonics			
S,s- Recognition			
S- Phonics			
P,p- Recognition			
P- Phonics			
W,w- Recognition			
W- Phonics			
J,j- Recognition			
J- Phonics			
K,k- Recognition			
K- Phonics			
Q,q- Recognition			
Q,- Phonics			
X,x- Recognition			
X- Phonics			

Y,y- Recognition			
Y,y- Phonics			
Z,z- Recognition			
Z- Phonics			

Word Recognition (Ages 4 & 5 only)

Word	Transpiring	Progressing	Accomplished
Go			
Dog			
Dad			
A			
It			
Cat			
To			
My			
Mom			
I			
Are			
For			
Me			
Big			
And			
Run			

Word	Transpiring	Progressing	Accomplished
Can			
Here			
The			
Is			
Said			
Up			
Word	**Transpiring**	**Progressing**	**Accomplished**
Not			
Away			
We			
Come			
Down			
See			
Little			
Look			
Play			
Make			
In			
Red			
Where			
Blue			
Find			
Yellow			

You			
Funny			
Jump			
Help			
One			
Two			
Three			

Social/Emotional (Age 3)

Skill	Transpiring	Progressing	Accomplished
Copies adults & Friends			
Shows affection for friends w/out prompting			
Takes turn in games			
Shows concern for crying friend			
Understands the idea of "mine" and "his" or "hers"			
Shows a wide range of emotions			
Separates easily from mom and dad			
May get upset with major changes in routine			
Dresses and undresses self			

Social/Emotional (Age 4)

Skill	Transpiring	Progressing	Accomplished
Enjoys doing new things			
Plays "Mom" and "Dad"			
Is more and more creative with			

make-believe play			
Cooperates with other children			
Often can't tell what's real and what's make-believe			
Talks about what she likes and what she is interested in			

Social/Emotional (Age 5)

Skill	Transpiring	Progressing	Accomplished
Wants to please friends			
Wants to be like friends			
More likely to agree with rules			
Likes to sing, dance, act			
Is aware of gender			
Can tell what's real and what's make-believe			
Shows more independence			
Is sometimes demanding and sometimes very cooperative			

Language/Communication (Age 3)

Skill	Transpiring	Progressing	Accomplished
Follows instructions with 2-3 steps			
Can name familiar things			
Understands words like "in", "on", and "under"			
Says first name, age, and sex			
Can name a friend			
Says words like "I", "me", "we", and "you" and some plurals (cars, dogs)			
Talks well enough for strangers to understand most of the time			

Carries on a conversation using 2 to 3 sentences			

Language/Communication (Age 4)

Skill	Transpiring	Progressing	Accomplished
Knows some basic rules of grammar, such as correctly using "he" and "she"			
Sings a song or says a poem from memory such as "Itsy Bitsy Spider" or the "Wheels on the Bus"			
Tells stories			
Can say first and last name			

Language/Communication (Age 5)

Skill	Transpiring	Progressing	Accomplished
Speaks very clearly			
Tells a simple story using full sentences			
Uses future tense; for example, "Grandma will be here."			
Says name and address			

Cognitive (learning, thinking, problem-solving) (Age 3)

Skill	Transpiring	Progressing	Accomplished
Can work toys with buttons, levers, & moving parts			
Can make-believe with dolls, animals, and people			
Does puzzles with 3 or 4 pieces			
Understands what "two" means			
Copies a circle with pencil or crayon			
Turns book pages one at a time			

Builds towers of more than 6 blocks			
Screws and unscrews jar lids or turns door handle			

Cognitive (learning, thinking, problem-solving) (Age 4)

Skill	Transpiring	Progressing	Accomplished
Names some colors and some numbers			
Understands the idea of counting			
Starts to understand time			
Remembers parts of a story			
Understands the idea of "same" or "different"			
Draws a person with 2 to 4 body parts			
Uses Scissors			
Starts to copy some capital letters			
Plays board or card games			
Tells you what he thinks is going to happen next in a book			

Cognitive (Learning, thinking, problem-solving) (Age 5)

Skill	Transpiring	Progressing	Accomplished
Counts 10 or more things			
Can draw a person with at least 6 body parts			
Can print some letters or numbers			
Copies a triangle and other geometric shapes			
Knows about things used daily, like food & phone			

Movement/Physical Development (Age 3)

Skill	Transpiring	Progressing	Accomplished
Climbs well			
Runs easily			
Pedals a tricycle (3-wheel bike)			
Walks up and down stairs, one foot on each step			

Movement/Physical Development (Age 4)

Skill	Transpiring	Progressing	Accomplished
Hops and stands on one foot up to 2 seconds			
Catches a bounced ball most of the time			
Pours, cuts with supervision, and mashes own food			

Movement/Physical Development (Age 5)

Skill	Transpiring	Progressing	Accomplished
Stands on one foot for 10 seconds or longer			
Hops, may be able to skip			
Can do a somersault			
Uses a fork and spoon and sometimes a table knife			
Can use the toilet on her own			
Swings and climbs			

Printed in Great Britain
by Amazon

40881026R00185